EARLY CHILDHOOD MOVEMENT ACTIVITIES ON A BUDGET

Renée M. McCall, MS, CAPE

North Syracuse Early Education Program

Diane H. Craft, PhD

State University of New York, College at Cortland

Library of Congress Cataloging-in-Publication Data

McCall, Renée M., 1958-
Purposeful play : early childhood movement activities on a budget / Renée M. McCall, Diane H. Craft.
p. cm.
Includes bibliographical references.
ISBN 0-7360-4641-0 (soft cover)
1. Movement education. 2. Early childhood education--Activity programs. I. Craft, Diane H., 1950- II. Title.
GV452.M35 2004
: 372.86'8--dc22
2003023847

ISBN: 0-7360-4641-0

The Web addresses cited in this text were current as of January 2004, unless otherwise noted.

Acquisitions Editor: Bonnie Pettifor; **Developmental Editor:** Amy Stahl; **Assistant Editors:** Amanda Gunn, Carla Zych, and Bethany Bentley; **Copyeditor:** Patsy Fortney; **Proofreader:** Kim Thoren; **Permission Manager:** Dalene Reeder; **Graphic Designer:** Fred Starbird; **Graphic Artist:** Kathleen Boudreau-Fuoss; **Photo Managers:** Kareema McLendon and Kelly Huff; **Cover Designer:** Andrea Souflée; **Photographer (cover):** John Miller; **Photographer (interior):** John Miller, unless otherwise noted; **Art Manager:** Kelly Hendren; **Illustrator:** Argosy; **Printer:** Versa Press

We thank the North Syracuse Early Education Program in North Syracuse, New York, for assistance in providing the location for the photo shoot for this book.

Printed in the United States of America 10 9 8 7 6 5 4 3 2 1

Human Kinetics
Web site: www.HumanKinetics.com

United States: Human Kinetics
P.O. Box 5076, Champaign, IL 61825-5076
800-747-4457
e-mail: humank@hkusa.com

Canada: Human Kinetics
475 Devonshire Road Unit 100
Windsor, ON N8Y 2L5
800-465-7301 (in Canada only)
e-mail: orders@hkcanada.com

Europe: Human Kinetics
107 Bradford Road, Stanningley
Leeds LS28 6AT, United Kingdom
+44 (0) 113 255 5665
e-mail: hk@hkeurope.com

Australia: Human Kinetics
57A Price Avenue, Lower Mitcham
South Australia 5062
08 8277 1555
e-mail: liaw@hkaustralia.com

New Zealand: Human Kinetics
Division of Sports Distributors NZ Ltd.
P.O. Box 300 226 Albany
North Shore City, Aukland
0064 9 448 1207
e-mail: blairc@hknewz.com

To my parents,
Richard and Marian Marchand.
You have both always been
an incredible inspiration to me,
a support system and model
to what unconditional love really is.
I love you both.

—Renée M. McCall

To my husband, Craig,
and children, Laura and David,
for your continuing love and support.

—Diane H. Craft

Contents

Game Finder

ACTIVITY COST KEY

$ = free or supercheap (under $5)
$$ = cheap ($5-15)
$$$ = moderate ($15-30)
$$$$ = expensive (more than $30; lower-cost materials are suggested in the activities)

Activity name	Page number	Activity cost	Curricular Goals								Holiday themes	Language and literacy
			Cardiovascular endurance	Spatial relationships	Locomotor skills	Motor planning	Muscular strength and endurance	Object, color, and shape recognition	Object control	Stability		
52 Pickup	53	$$			x			x	x			x
Air Ball	91	$$	x									
Apples in the Tree	106	$			x			x		x	x	x
Bubble Wrap Mail Delivery	42	$$		x	x	x		x			x	x
Carl the Construction Worker	96	$$				x			x		x	x
Cheap Skate	44	$	x			x				x	x	
Day at the Beach, A	186	$$$$			x	x			x			x
Day on the Ocean, A	183	$$$$			x	x	x		x			
Day in Bike Village, A	138	$$ + trikes	x	x		x	x	x			x	x
Follow the Brightly Lit Road	93	$$		x	x	x						
Fruit Salad	82	$$							x			
Go Fish	58	$$					x				x	
Going to the Zoo	113	$			x			x				x
Heartbeat	156	$$	x									
Jumping the Hurdles	74	$			x			x			x	

Let's Make a Meal	114	$			x			x			x	x
Mealtime	167	$			x			x				x
Mitten Match	117	$			x			x			x	
Nets, Targets, and Balls	65	$$							x			
Pizza	108	$			x			x				x
Pumpkin Bowling	84	$ + climber					x		x		x	
Pumpkins Galore	86	$$$			x	x	x	x	x		x	x
Racquetball Fun With Hangers	48	$							x			
Ride for Life	143	$ + trikes	x			x	x					
Roll Out the Bubble Wrap	39	$ for 4 5-ft rolls	x		x						x	
Salad Run	164	$$			x			x				x
Salad Spinner	161	$	x		x							x
Scoop It Up	46	$							x			
Scooter Pull	62	$ + scooters					x				x	
Smiley Face	103	$			x			x				x
Sport Ball	119	$			x			x			x	x
Supermarket Sweep	111	$$			x			x				x
Suspended Noodle Jump	77	$$	x		x						x	
Swing Your Noodle Bat	71	$							x			
You've Got Mail	134	$	x	x		x	x	x			x	x
Walking Blocks	50	$		x						x	x	

Preface

Creating an exciting movement program for young children at minimal cost can be a thoroughly enjoyable and rewarding experience. Children are natural movers; they are always looking for new ways to learn and understand their environment as they move. Because children are wonderfully imaginative, you do not need expensive equipment to entice them to move. This book strives to inspire you to use your own imagination and inexpensive materials to create enriched, purposeful play—movement games and activities that excite children and inspire them to move in ways that provide planned physical benefits as well as cognitive learning experiences.

The games and activities in *Purposeful Play* use the following:

- Pumpkins, milk cartons, and socks to help the children develop fundamental motor skills
- Theme cards made from laminated card stock, each of which contains a picture and the word describing it
- Cones, pulleys, and eyebolts to help children develop fitness
- Plastic fruits and vegetables and big books to help children learn nutrition concepts
- A 55-foot inflatable whale to help children learn integrated curriculum concepts
- Music to add even more fun to all of these activities!

These activities are designed to work in a wide variety of real-world learning environments that might seem less than ideal for conducting a movement program. These activities can be used even if you have

- limited funds with which to buy equipment,
- a small indoor space or only an outdoor area in which to conduct the movement program,
- only a few minutes in which to set up equipment, and
- children who need novelty to be motivated to move.

In addition, we believe that quality movement programs are much more than just getting children to exercise. In our first book, *Moving With a Purpose* (McCall and Craft 2000), which is the companion book to *Purposeful Play,* we explained why movement is essential to young children's optimal development and how to use a child-centered approach in a movement program. We emphasized developmentally appropriate practices that include children with special needs. Perhaps most important, we stressed how to offer a comprehensive curriculum in which activities are selected based not on the whim of the teacher, but on whether they can help children achieve specific educational goals and objectives. Now, *Purposeful Play* continues this developmentally appropriate, child-centered, inclusive approach to conducting a movement program.

Readers of *Moving With a Purpose,* and those who have attended the many presentations and workshops we have conducted based on that book, have asked us for more information addressing how to offer a quality movement program that requires only inexpensive materials. Our response was to write *Purposeful Play* to share many of the new and inexpensive movement activities developed by Renée McCall in the North Syracuse Early Education Program. We also wrote this book to share lesson plans and curriculum resources that teach young children important bike safety, fitness, and nutrition concepts in addition to motor skill development. Finally, we wanted to share ways of enhancing language, literacy, and other aspects of the cognitive domain within a movement program.

We designed *Purposeful Play* to assist adults working in different settings with three- to seven-year-old children of all abilities. The book is written with five audiences in mind:

- Preschool teachers and family child care providers
- Physical educators and elementary educators
- Early childhood educators; adapted physical educators; and physical, occupational, and speech therapists in school-based preschool programs
- Adults who direct after-school programs
- Teachers and parents in settings that include young children with special needs

This book is a practical, well-organized resource full of teacher-tested and child-approved movement activities presented in a user-friendly, easy-to-read format. We hope these activities will enable you—whether you are a new or experienced teacher—to enhance your movement program with developmentally appropriate and inclusive activities—on a budget!

Acknowledgments

I would like to thank my dear friend and coworker of close to two decades, Diane Chermak, for being the person she is. Our award-winning Adapted Physical Education Department is a result of very focused and committed teamwork. I would like to thank my principal, Dr. Kathleen Esposito, for her continued support of adapted physical education and the importance of gross motor programs at the preschool level. To the staff at the North Syracuse Early Education Program, thank you for making coming to work each day a pleasure. To Julie Daniel, thank you for your contribution to this book and for the time you spend teaching us how to most effectively work on addressing a child's speech and language development while in the gymnasium. To Diane Craft, my coauthor, thank you for a journey that I hope will enrich many lives. And to my daughter, Katie, who never once complained about my long hours working or time away from home, but instead helped in any way she could. Thank you. You're the best!

—Renée M. McCall

Thank you to my coauthor, Renée McCall, for generously sharing her excellent teaching activities and ideas found on the pages of this book. Thank you also to Michele Gonzales for sharing her literacy expertise; Cindy Bagby for recommending children's stories about bikes, nutrition, and whales; and Beth Biersdorf for critiquing the chapter on music. Finally, an enormous thank-you to Craig for his insightful comments on earlier drafts of this book and for caring for our children while I was writing.

—Diane H. Craft

We both wish to thank John Miller, our photographer, for another round of beautiful pictures. Thank you also to Human Kinetics, especially Bonnie Pettifor for inviting us to write this book and Amy Stahl for ushering the book through the many developmental steps with skillful attention to detail.

How to Use This Book

Purposeful Play is a survival guide for teachers who know movement is important for young children, yet may not have access to a gymnasium or expensive equipment with which to offer a traditional comprehensive physical education curriculum. This book is designed to provide structured movement activities that are not expensive, yet are effective in helping children ages three to seven become skillful movers. The activities use predominantly inexpensive equipment and require minimal space. They are often enriched movement activities, in that they are designed to encourage collateral learning in the cognitive domain as they are played.

The Move and Match activities in chapter 9 are especially well suited to reinforce academic concepts that require identification and categorization. One example is the Move and Match game Shape Up. Children practice a variety of locomotor movements such as jumping, walking backward, and running as they move between points A and B. The object is to find the paper square, triangle, or circle at point B and bring it back to point A, once again using locomotor movements. This simple game presents many opportunities to help children learn cognitive concepts such as object, color, and shape recognition. Substitute letters for shapes, and children begin to learn letter recognition. Print simple words on cards, and now children practice beginning reading as they move. The opportunities to infuse cognitive learning, especially language and literacy, within this enriched movement game are endless. Refer to the Game Finder at the beginning of the book for a list of activities that lend themselves to practicing language and literacy skills. We have placed an icon in the margin next to each activity or variation that may be especially helpful in teaching and reinforcing emerging language and literacy skills.

Each of the 36 activities in this book contains the following elements to provide quick and easy-to-understand explanations:

- **Curricular goals**. A list of the skills to be learned by playing the activity that is cross-referenced with the curricular goals in the Game Finder on pages viii-ix.
- **Overview**. A quick summary of how the activity is played.
- **Goals for children**. A short explanation of all that children can learn by playing this activity.
- **Equipment**. A list of the equipment needed for playing this activity.

* **Equipment tips**. Explanations of where to find equipment or lower-cost alternatives for the suggested equipment.

- **Preparation**. Instructions for how to make equipment or set up the learning environment.

- **Instructions**. Step-by-step explanations of how to teach the activity.
- **Adaptations**. Ideas for modifying the activity to accommodate children with special needs.
- **Variations**. Ideas for making the activity more challenging for older or more skillful children. Ideas for changing the activity theme to suit a holiday, to develop language and literacy, or to meet other cognitive goals are offered.
- **Changing the space**. Ideas for how to accommodate the activity to smaller spaces or outdoor areas.

We designed this book to help you select activities based on their educational purpose. We suggest beginning your lesson planning by identifying the curricular goals that you would like your students to learn. Where practical, select from among the curricular goals in the Game Finder. Then scan the column under each curricular goal you selected to find those activities designed to teach the specific curricular goal. Next, turn to the activity in the book and read our suggestions for doing the activity. Following these steps ensures that you are planning purposeful play by selecting activities based on their educational purpose.

Purposeful Play is written in three parts. Part I is full of ideas for organizing your movement program. Chapter 1 begins with a scenario that highlights the features and benefits of this book. It is followed by an explanation of our philosophical orientation and suggestions for building an early childhood movement program for children three to seven years of age. We also offer suggestions for teaching activities in ways that children can be successful.

Chapter 2 offers suggestions for acquiring the equipment needed for conducting the activities in this book. It discusses repurposing available play equipment; scouring basements, attics, and garages for more items; seeking donations from friends and colleagues; and purchasing inexpensive supplies at discount stores. The chapter concludes with several practical suggestions for using and storing equipment to allow for quick setup of activities in the future.

Chapter 3 explores ways to use music effectively to enhance movement lesson plans. We include ideas for selecting appropriate music, whether using dictated movement, chants, or background music. Specific titles and their sources are recommended.

Part II presents explanations and instructions for activities and many variations to use in the classroom, in the gymnasium, or on the playground. These activities are organized into chapters based on the inexpensive equipment they require. Chapter 4 presents starter activities for your movement program, each requiring materials that can be purchased for $5 or less. Chapter 5 explains novel uses of ropes, pulleys, and eyebolts for movement activities designed to develop upper body strength and improve visual tracking skills. Chapter 6 features activities using foam pool noodles in ways ideally suited to young children. Chapter 7 suggests using real, plastic, or fabric fruits and vegetables instead of conventional balls in several imaginative, fun activities. Chapter 8 shows innovative ways you can use vinyl house gutters and elbows in movement activities. Finally, chapter 9 presents eight activities that involve moving from one point to another, making a match, and returning to the starting point. These Move and Match activities are wonderful ways to teach the academic concepts of matching shapes, colors, and objects, and reinforcing number and language and literacy skills such as letter and word recognition.

Part III moves beyond simple activities to discuss larger-scale programs and special events you may want to implement in your curriculum to bring recognition to your movement program. Chapter 10 presents a comprehensive curriculum for teaching cycling skills and safety to young children, whether they are riding tricycles or bicycles. Lesson plans explain how to teach these skills and concepts in exciting, safe ways. Sources for purchasing low-cost bike helmets are included along with recommendations for bike safety curriculum kits.

Chapter 11 offers practical ideas for teaching basic concepts about fitness and nutrition. Through these ideas, children as young as three years of age can begin to learn about their bodies and the physical activities and foods that can help keep their bodies healthy. Given the epidemic of obesity among children in the United States, the lesson plans and curriculum resources offered in this chapter are important for teachers everywhere to use in educating young children about healthy eating and exercise habits.

Chapter 12 introduces Lucy, a 55-foot inflatable whale who can "come alive" in five minutes using a basic two-foot by two-foot floor fan for inflation. You can construct this highly motivating teaching tool for under $100 using packing tape, two large rolls of plastic, and instructions purchased on the Web from her creators at Wheelock College. Although not inexpensive to construct, Lucy is durable. She can be used for many years to present innovative, integrated curricula in movement, reading, math, and ecology.

Chapter 13 takes a more global view of movement programs, offering high-visibility special event activities to promote your program. The chapter explains how to conduct 10 program promotion events, including the following:

- Open house to showcase the movement program
- Ride for Life fund-raiser
- Parent–child "Take a Day to Play" campaign
- End-of-the-year dance party

These and other exciting events bring wonderful movement experiences to children and community recognition to your movement program.

Part I

Organizing for Purposeful Play

Part I is written to help you organize a movement program that is developmentally appropriate, inclusive, and focused on learning. Chapter 1 provides general guidelines for teaching movement activities in ways that challenge young children, yet also provide for their success. In chapter 2 we offer global suggestions for acquiring, setting up, and storing equipment; these suggestions are especially helpful when time and funds are limited. Finally, chapter 3 is full of useful suggestions for incorporating music into your movement program. We also include extensive lists of CD titles and their sources to guide your purchases.

chapter 1

Teaching Purposeful Play Activities

Aventika is sitting at her desk musing as she flips through the equipment catalog she just retrieved from her mailbox. She gazes longingly at page after page of large, colorful, motivating, and expensive equipment. She dreams of using all of this wonderful equipment in her early childhood movement program. Setting the catalog aside, she rereads a memo that was also in today's mail. The memo outlines the education budget cuts to her program, effective immediately. She knows that ordering the wonderful equipment on the catalog pages is not going to happen this year and may not happen next year either.

Aventika bites her lower lip in frustration. She wants to expand her movement program but doesn't know where to start. She senses the increasing boredom of the young children she teaches. Movement activities that were once new and exciting to them are becoming uninteresting because she is repeating them too frequently. With each passing week, she experiences increasing behavior problems among the children, which she suspects are a result of her stagnating curriculum.

And then there is the issue of space. She has only a small activity area in which to conduct the movement program. Sometimes she does not even have this space, instead needing to conduct movement lessons in classrooms or outside in the play area.

Aventika knows that she must find ways to conduct novel, motivating activities that meet the needs of her young students. Yet she must do this on a shoestring budget—or find other sources of funding. In addition, she needs to be able to do these activities in small spaces with limited setup time. Aventika needs some new ideas and activities for her movement program—and she needs them now. Where will she turn?

After school she stops by the local child care center to pick up her daughter. She mentions her frustration to her daughter's teacher, Davida, who also believes that a quality movement program is important for young children. Davida explains that she has devised a movement program that uses inexpensive equipment in novel ways because she also has almost no budget for equipment purchases. She uses novel, inexpensive materials such as bubble wrap; plastic spoons and bags; ropes, pulleys, and eyebolts; strings of holiday lights; and vinyl house gutters. Using these materials, Davida has found ways to teach a variety of fundamental movement skills such as throwing, catching, striking, and rolling, along with running, hopping, jumping, and sliding. She also uses the equipment in movement activities that develop fitness, cognitive concepts, and language and literacy skills. Intrigued, Aventika asks her to explain how she does this.

WE'VE WRITTEN THIS BOOK to share equipment and movement activity ideas as remedies for the frustration Aventika and others in similar circumstances may feel, including you. It is our intent to provide novel, exciting, and motivating movement activities designed to keep the interest of the young children you teach, enrich their cognitive learning, and build the reputation of your program—all on a limited budget.

The movement activities outlined in this book have the following characteristics:

- **They are motivating.** These activities motivate young children by offering novelty, variety, and opportunities to imitate adult tasks; freedom to make their own choices; and chances to move and play with joyful enthusiasm.
- **They use low-cost equipment.** The times in which we live are, more often than not, characterized by budget cuts. We need to become more resourceful as educators to get the maximum value from our budget money. If you are on a shoestring budget, you will appreciate the many activities we've included that can be performed with equipment purchased at dollar or discount stores or made from materials commonly found at home. We have also included suggestions for other ways to acquire equipment through donations and fund-raising.
- **They can be done in small spaces or outdoors.** If you have access to a large gymnasium, you can easily conduct the activities in this book. Yet many of these activities can also be adapted to small spaces or be conducted in an outdoor play area. Read the section titled "Changing the Space" following each activity for ideas on how to conduct the activity in a classroom or outdoor play area.
- **They are quick to set up.** Many of the activities in this book require only a few minutes to set up and take down. As such, they are perfect if you are teaching in a classroom or a gymnasium that has to be cleared of equipment before the next class. After installing readily available hardware in the activity area just once, you will be able to set up seemingly complex activities in just a few minutes each time thereafter.

- **They enrich children's cognitive learning.** These activities enrich the learning of cognitive concepts such as identification and classification concepts, spatial relations, and basic language and literacy skills.

What you are about to read is the compilation of nearly two decades of Renée McCall's experience teaching physical education to preschool children. Renée has taught these activities in gymnasiums as well as typical classrooms, small homes, and outdoors. Physical educators have used them in elementary physical education programs. Early childhood educators and elementary educators have used them in classrooms and on the playground. Physical, occupational, and speech therapists have used them in therapy rooms and in gymnasiums during children's physical education classes. Family child care providers have used them in their homes and yards. We are optimistic that many of these activities will work well in your early childhood movement program.

PHILOSOPHICAL ORIENTATION

Now let's consider the philosophical orientation behind the activities in *Purposeful Play*. We, the authors, value teaching movement activities that are

- developmentally appropriate,
- inclusive of children with special needs, and
- focused on learning.

Let's consider each of these three philosophical orientations in turn.

Implementing Developmentally Appropriate Practices

The activities in this book are developmentally appropriate for children three to seven years of age. These activities reflect the guidelines for Appropriate Practices in Movement Programs for Young Children Ages 3-5 by the National Association for Sport and Physical Education (NASPE) (2000) as summarized in "For Physical Educators."

These activities can also help young children achieve the NASPE standards. The information in "National Association for Sport & Physical Education (NASPE) *National Standards for Physical Education—*Kindergarten" may be especially helpful for physical educators who need to prepare their young students to meet these national standards.

For Physical Educators

The activities in this book can be used to help each child in your movement program become *physically educated.* According to the National Association for Sport & Physical Education (NASPE, 2000, 5), a physically educated person

- has learned skills necessary to perform a variety of physical activities;
- is physically fit;
- participates regularly in physical activity;
- knows the implications of, and the benefits from, involvement in physical activities; [and]
- values physical activity and its contribution to a healthy lifestyle.

NASPE lists five premises for developmentally appropriate practices with young children. The NASPE statements are in bold (2000, 6-7), followed with an explanation of how the activities in this book are responsive to paraphrased NASPE statements.

1. **Three-, four- and, five-year-old children are different from elementary school-aged children.** These activities are designed to provide young children with extensive opportunities to explore and experiment with movement to develop mature fundamental movement patterns.
2. **Young children learn through interaction with their environment.** These activities are designed to have all children active most, if not all, of the time during the movement lesson.
3. **Teachers of young children are guides or facilitators.** These activities are designed to create an environment that will entice children to learn specific objectives while you, the teacher, facilitate their learning.
4. **Young children learn and develop in an integrated fashion.** These activities are designed to help children learn movement skills at the same time that they are learning cognitive and affective skills.
5. **Planned movement experiences enhance play experiences.** Free play on the playground or in the designated gross motor room is necessary but insufficient for children to become physically educated. These activities are designed to aid you in establishing or enhancing a movement program that offers a wide variety of fundamental movement skills. This book does not contain elementary school games that have been watered down to fit younger children. Rather, these activities were conceived and refined based on the needs and interests of young children, with an emphasis on exploration and experimentation with movement, rather than skill refinement.

National Association for Sport & Physical Education (NASPE) National Standards for Physical Education

Each NASPE standard is printed in bold (National Association for Sport & Physical Education 2004, 9), followed by our explanation of how you can use this book's activities to help young children achieve each standard. Refer to the curricular goals listed for each activity and cross-referenced in the Game Finder to identify the many activities that help children meet a standard.

1. **Demonstrates competency in motor skills and movement patterns needed to perform a variety of physical activities.** Many of this book's activities provide children practice in fundamental motor skills so they may evolve toward mature patterns. The activities that address the curricular goals "locomotor skills," "object control skills," and "stability" are especially well suited to helping children develop these mature patterns.
2. **Demonstrates understanding of movement concepts, principles, strategies, and tactics as they apply to the learning and performance of physical activities.** The Move and Match activities in chapter 9 are particularly well suited to teaching children the names and movements of locomotor patterns as they move between points A and B. These games also help teach spatial relationships and moving in different pathways and directions and at different levels and ranges. Just about any of the activities in this book can be used to facilitate individual children's movements, helping them learn the basic cognitive concepts associated with movement, such as bending their knees as they land a jump. The activities in this book that address the curricular goals of "motor planning" and "spatial relationships" are also well suited to help children develop movement concepts and principles.
3. **Participates regularly in physical activity.** Each activity in this book has been refined so that it helps children experience joy and purpose in physical activity. The fitness and nutrition lesson plans and resources in chapter 11 are specifically designed to help children learn that eating healthy foods and participating regularly in physical activity is not only fun but also good for you.
4. **Achieves and maintains a health-enhancing level of physical fitness.** The activities in this book that address the curricular goals of "cardiovascular endurance and "muscular strength and endurance" are especially well suited to help children develop health-enhancing levels of physical fitness. Lesson plans in chapter 11 suggest activities to teach

(continued)

(continued)

children the physiological signs they can observe that are associated with exercising vigorously.

5. **Exhibits responsible personal and social behavior that respects self and others in physical activity settings.** Each of this book's activities can be used to help children learn responsible personal and social behaviors. These activities are developmentally appropriate for young children and thus encourage success. Successful movers are more likely to act appropriately, primarily because they are not frustrated or bored. Each activity is designed so children with special needs can participate alongside their typical peers. This inclusive approach helps develop understanding and respect for individual differences.
6. **Values physical activity for health, enjoyment, challenge, self-expression and/or social interaction.** All activities and teaching methods in this book are designed to help children experience joy and purpose in physical activity.

Reprinted from *Moving into the future: National standards for physical education: A guide to content* (2004) with permission from the National Association for Sport and Physical Education (NASPE), 1900 Association Drive, Reston, VA 20191-1599.

Activities in this book are designed so children with special needs can participate alongside their typical peers.

Including Children With Special Needs

The activities in this book were developed in an adapted physical education program in which half of the students are typically developing and half have special needs, including intellectual and language delays; speech delays; visual impairments or deafness; pervasive developmental disorders; and physical impairments. These activities help all children learn, regardless of their abilities.

Perhaps the most important factor in the successful inclusion of children with such diverse and significant special needs is to adopt an attitude of acceptance. Teachers who truly welcome all children in the movement program will find a way to successfully include even the children with severe disabilities. Such teachers do not stop trying different adaptations until they find a way to allow every child to participate in each activity at his or her own level. Each activity includes a section titled "Adaptations" that offers specific ideas for including children with special needs. Adapted equipment can be very helpful for children who have limited mobility. Two examples of adapted equipment are pictured in figure 1.1.

Focusing on Learning

Too often movement activities for young children look more like free play—or are inspired by the adult's desire to keep them busy, happy, and well behaved. The focus of movement programs needs to be children *learning*! A well-constructed and well-delivered movement program provides so much more to young learners than simply the opportunity to "let off some steam." A quality movement program enhances the development of the whole child in the affective, cognitive, and motor domains. When you are developing a movement curriculum, a key step is deciding what you want the children to learn from the curriculum. While young children are moving, they are feeling, thinking, and learning to move skillfully. "These feelings and attitudes that children have while they move are part of what we call the affective domain . . . . The cognitive domain refers to knowing or perceiving. Through moving, children continuously learn about ideas . . . . The motor domain refers to movement. Through moving, children continually become more skillful movers" (McCall and Craft 2000, 11).* Following is our vision of early childhood movement curricular goals.

Quality movement programs address curricular goals in all three domains. In terms of the affective (feeling or emotional) domain, movement

*Reprinted, by permission, from R. McCall and D. Craft, 2000, *Moving with a purpose: Developing programs for pre-schoolers of all abilities* (Champaign, IL: Human Kinetics), 11.

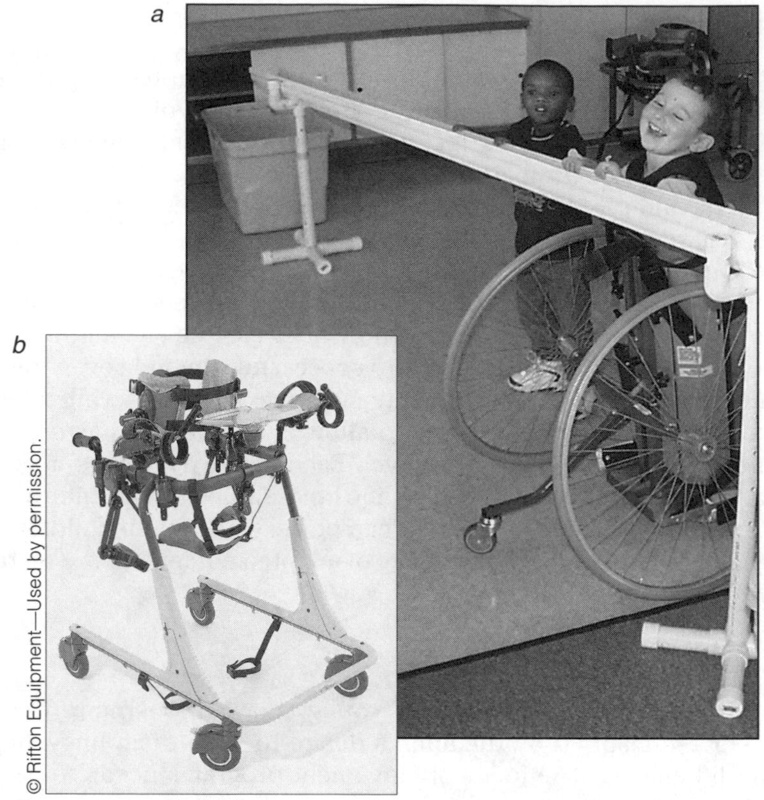

© Rifton Equipment—Used by permission.

Figure 1.1 Some children with special needs will require mobility equipment to participate in many games and activities: *(a)* Child using a mobile prone stander; and *(b)* a gait trainer.

Early Childhood Movement Curricular Goals

Preschool Movement Program Goals in the Affective Domain

- Strengthen the way children feel about themselves
  - Develop positive self-images and self-esteem
  - Develop self-motivation to become independent learners who confidently choose to be active
- Develop social skills
  - Learn to share, cooperate, and take turns
  - Learn to play safely and talk kindly
- Develop joyful and purposeful play

Preschool Movement Program Goals in the Cognitive Domain

- Learn how to communicate, enriching language and literacy skills
- Learn basic rules and game play
- Learn to follow instructions
- Learn to recognize objects, colors, and shapes
- Learn about body awareness
  - Identify body parts
  - Identify movement concepts
    - Effort (time, force, flow)
    - Space (self-space, general space, levels—high, low)
    - Relationships (of body parts, to objects—over, under, in front of, behind)

Preschool Movement Program Goals in the Motor Domain

- Learn rudimentary movement skills, if not already mastered
- Learn fundamental movement skills
  - Learn locomotor skills (walk, run, jump, gallop, hop, skip, leap)
  - Learn object control (throw, catch, kick, strike, bounce)
  - Learn stability (static and dynamic balance)
- Develop health-related physical fitness
  - Develop cardiovascular endurance
  - Develop muscular strength and endurance
- Develop motor planning (sequencing movements based on sensory input)
- Develop functional and generalizable adaptations of motor skills, as needed
- Learn to use recreational equipment—tricycles, roller racers, scooters, swings, adapted as needed to increase mobility

Reprinted, by permission, from R. McCall and D. Craft, 2000, *Moving with a purpose: Developing programs for preschoolers of all abilities* (Champaign, IL: Human Kinetics), 13.

activities provide excellent opportunities for children to develop positive feelings about themselves and others. You can help the children you teach develop in this area by sowing the seeds of good sport conduct at a young age.

Movement activities also provide wonderful opportunities to teach a variety of cognitive concepts, which refer to knowing or perceiving. Because they enjoy moving, children engaged in movement activities are exuberant and attentive and thus primed for learning cognitive concepts.

Language and Literacy

Movement activities, such as the Move and Match activities in chapter 9, are especially suited to teaching language and literacy skills. Consider what Julie Daniel, speech and language pathologist, had to say about working on children's communication during a movement lesson.

> Communication is an integral part of children's lives. It touches every aspect of their day including their interactions with peers, their understanding of what is going on around them and their ability to effect changes around them. Addressing a child's speech and language development must follow from the above assumptions. The skills taught must be functional and ideally are practiced in the context of typical settings. A motivated child who is engaged in motoric play is highly stimulable to learn many aspects of communication.
>
> The list of skills that could be introduced in a physical play environment is extensive and is limited only by your imagination. You will find success integrating the following communication skills in gross motor movement:
>
> - Building receptive and expressive vocabulary (what one understands and what one actually says) including verbs, vehicles, foods, occupations, animals, location words, and descriptors such as adjectives and adverbs
> - Answering wh-? questions such as, Who has the ____ (ball)?, Where is the ___ (toy or dog)? or Why did that happen?
> - Distinguishing same and different through tasks such as matching pictures and finding things that don't belong
> - Imitating actions, an important precursor to imitating speech
> - Building pragmatic skills such as turn taking; gaining attention in appropriate ways; using an appropriate tone of voice; using words, sign language, or picture symbols to have needs and wants met; using socially appropriate phrases including *excuse me* and *thank you*; requesting assistance in an appropriate manner; and acknowledging the communication bids of others
> - Building auditory memory skills such as following multiple-step instructions and bringing the correct requested item

- Improving speech intelligibility through practicing targeted sounds

> The integration of communication skills and gross motor activity is a unique way to expand a child's competence in critical areas of development. Always take advantage of these prime "teachable moments" to combine play and invaluable learning! (Julie Daniel, personal communication, August 10, 2003)

Refer to the Game Finder at the beginning of the book for a list of activities that lend themselves to practicing language and literacy skills. We have placed an icon in the margin next to each activity or variation that may be especially helpful in teaching and reinforcing emerging language and literacy skills.

Child-Centered Approach

A child-centered approach to teaching movement activities focuses on the needs and interests of each child, rather than the dictums of a rigid curriculum. The child-centered approach is characterized by child-initiated and teacher-facilitated activities. This approach is developmentally appropriate, motivates children, and minimizes behavior difficulties because it allows children to make choices during the activity, within an environment that the teacher has created. Many of the activities in this book are conducive to using a child-centered approach to teaching.

Prior to the lesson, you determine the goals for children and carefully create the movement environment to help children achieve these goals. During the lesson, your job is to give instructions and monitor the activity for safety, but your students may decide what, when, and how they will participate in the activity. You are then free to facilitate the children's movement performance in the activities they have chosen.

Consider this example of a child-centered approach to teaching. You have assessed the children's skills and decide to teach object control through today's movement activity. You set up several targets at varying distances from a net strung across an open space. Children stand behind the net beside bins of balls they can throw over the net at the targets. All children are free to choose which types of balls to throw, which target to aim at, and whether and when they may move to another target. The activity is designed to safely run itself with only general adult supervision. This structure frees you to facilitate individual children's movements. You might prompt a child to begin with the ball up next to her ear to get a windup, prompt another one to step as he throws, and prompt a third to look right at the target as she throws.

Many of the activities in this book can be conducted as stations, in which children are free to move from one station to another during the lesson. This format allows children to decide which, if any, station they want to work at, how long they want to work there, and if and when they want to go to another station. Other activities in this book require that you give more instruction (in particular the Move and Match activities in chapter 9). In the Move and Match activities you give the children specific instructions about the objects they are to locate and match. Wherever possible, try to provide the children with choices within the Move and Match activities, including whether they want to participate at all. Of course, you will want to learn why a child chooses not to participate in any activity and plan an approach that will eventually help the child feel comfortable enough to want to participate.

BUILDING A MOVEMENT PROGRAM

Find out how you can create and use a comprehensive movement curriculum in this book's companion text, *Moving With a Purpose* (McCall and Craft 2000). In *Moving With a Purpose* you will find a more complete explanation of what children can learn through a movement curriculum, along with an easy-to-understand explanation of how to develop a movement program curriculum. Best of all, the book *Moving With a Purpose* presents 54 additional movement activities and a sample 40-week preschool movement curriculum to get you started. Be sure that the movement activities you teach offer children a rich variety of movement experiences to help them develop in all three domains.

Begin to build a movement program by first assessing the skills and interests of your students as well as the available facilities and equipment. (Refer to *Moving With a Purpose* for information about assessing the fundamental motor skills of young children as a basis for planning curricula and lessons.) Next, develop a curriculum that includes written curricular goals you want the children to achieve during the course of the program. Consider spiraling the goals throughout the year by planning activities that address each of the goals in turn over the weeks of instruction. Then spiral back to revisit goals already addressed earlier in the year. As an example, you may decide to focus on object control during the second, fifth, and ninth weeks of the year. A curriculum that continually returns to each of the curricular goals provides children with extensive, repeated practice in a wide variety of skills. Then develop lesson plans for the movement program to help children achieve these curricular goals.

Now it is time to plan how you will teach movement activities. We recommend that you do the following when you teach (McCall and Craft 2000):

- **Create a welcoming environment.** Create a movement area that sparks children's interests by hanging posters on the walls and decorating the area with attractive cartoon characters.
- **Establish routines** for lessons. We use the following format: warm-up, introduction of the lesson's concepts, activities to practice skills, and cool-down with a lesson summary. Examples of lesson plans are presented in chapters 10 and 11.
- **Use music as a cue** to start and stop activity. Children can quickly learn that they may begin an activity when they hear the music and are to stop the activity when the music stops. Refer to chapter 3 for more information on using music in movement activities.
- **Establish clear boundaries** that convey to children where they may and may not go. Young children can more easily understand boundaries that are marked by ropes and mats than by painted lines or tape on the floor.
- **Conduct open-ended activities** that allow for the experimentation and exploration described earlier, rather than rigid requirements for conformity that are likely to frustrate teachers and children alike. Open-ended activities allow for more than one way of performing a skill. Providing a variety of targets at varying distances and permitting children to throw at targets of their choice when they wish is an example of an open-ended activity.

Lesson Planning

Consider the following as a generic structure for a 30-minute movement lesson. Adjust the times and number of activities to suit your situation.

- Warm-up exercises to dictated music, which are songs with directions included (5 minutes)
- Explain movement activity or stations (2 minutes)
- Lead movement activity (20 minutes)
- Cool-down and lesson summary (3 minutes)

Warming up, exercising vigorously, and cooling down in each class can lead children to develop a lifelong habit for physical activity. Note that lessons on bike safety or fitness and nutrition may also include time to introduce cognitive concepts after the warm-up and before the movement activity. We recommend ending a movement activity at the height of excitement, before children's interest begins to wane. In this way they will be eager to play the activity again in future lessons.

Themes for Motivation

We encourage you to have a theme for each lesson, such as fishing for paper fish; shopping for fruits and vegetables; matching cars; imitating Carl the construction worker; or any other appropriate theme you can imagine. Use this theme to generate and maintain children's interest in the activity. Also use the theme to positively redirect children who are off task by asking a question that requires them to find an object or perform a task that relates to the activity's theme.

Vary the theme each time you repeat a specific movement activity. Throw plastic balls at targets this week; next time change the activity to throwing real potatoes into a container to make potato salad; the following time throw paper balls at a fabric target of a favorite cartoon character. In each case, children are practicing throwing, but the theme is varied so the activity remains fresh and appealing.

One of the easiest ways to add a theme to movement activities is through the use of theme cards. These are laminated plain-paper cards showing a picture of an object and the word for the object printed next to it. They are used as objects to be gathered or matched. Read about how to make theme cards in chapter 2.

TEACHING FOR CHILDREN'S SUCCESS

One of the most important guidelines in teaching movement is to *provide repetition until mastery; then increase the challenge.* Plan movement lessons to provide many opportunities for children to practice a new skill. Once they have mastered the skill, change the activity to make the skill more challenging. This helps children learn while minimizing frustration or boredom.

Another guideline in planning lessons that are challenging but not overwhelming is to *change the task until a child is successful at least 75 percent of the time.* Consider an example in which a child is throwing a plastic fruit into a container from behind a barrier several feet away. If the child is getting the fruit into the container about every three out of four attempts, then the task may be ideal for the child's present skill level. But if the child gets the fruit in the container only once or twice out of four attempts, then it may be time to simplify the task by either moving the child closer to the container or substituting a larger container. Children who are challenged, yet successful, most of the time are likely to enjoy the activity and want to continue practicing. This is what we aim to achieve when we plan and conduct lessons.

A third guideline concerns giving feedback to children: *Strive to provide at least four positive comments to every one negative comment.* This maintains a positive teaching environment that is enjoyable for everyone.

If you find you are correcting children more than just a few times during a lesson, it is time to change your lesson. Think of other ways you can structure the activity so children will not be tempted to do the things to which you need to say no.

Each of the activities in this book has been teacher tested for several years with children of widely varying abilities. Each activity has been refined until it works successfully and follows the three guidelines outlined in this section. It is our hope that you will be able to benefit from the experience of Renée McCall as you try these same activities, refining them as needed to work in your own setting. We are optimistic that you will find a wealth of ideas to enrich your movement program on the following pages.

chapter 2

Acquiring Equipment for Purposeful Play

Jackie has been a teacher of young children for many years. Each year she likes to add a new emphasis to her curriculum. This year she wants to focus on expanding and improving the movement opportunities for the young children in her class. She has always used dictated movement songs and has an extensive collection of CDs. Beyond her CD collection, she doesn't have any other equipment with which to teach movement. Or does she?

Jackie observes a child crawling under a table to retrieve a toy and realizes that if she draped a sheet over it, the table could serve as a tunnel. She watches another child throw a small ball of yarn she had reserved for an art project and recognizes that the yarn would make a safe ball for throwing indoors. She excitedly scans the room, noticing the waffle blocks, crates, hula hoops, plastic fruits, and many other play items. She smiles as she realizes that she already has a plethora of equipment waiting to be repurposed for use in her movement program.

ACQUIRING EQUIPMENT FOR A MOVEMENT PROGRAM can be a challenge for Jackie and many teachers. This chapter provides a brief overview of four ways to acquire movement program equipment for little expense. It also provides suggestions for quick and easy equipment setup and storage. The "Resources" section at the end of this chapter lists several sources for purchasing equipment. In addition to the equipment ideas in this chapter, each activity throughout this book also has a section titled "Equipment Tips" that offers suggestions for acquiring or making the specific equipment needed for that activity. Yes, it *is* possible to teach movement activities on a low budget.

ACQUIRING EQUIPMENT

We suggest four ways of acquiring equipment needed for teaching the movement activities in this book.

- Use, or repurpose, equipment you already have.
- Make your own equipment.
- Ask for donations of needed equipment.
- Buy inexpensive equipment at a discount department store or dollar store.

A discussion of each way follows.

Repurposing Equipment You Already Have

First, let's consider how you might be able to use equipment you already have on hand. Consider repurposing plastic fruits and vegetables that might be in the kitchen center of a preschool or kindergarten classroom for the Roll a Veggie, Toss a Fruit activities in chapter 7. Use these same fruits and vegetables in the Move and Match game Supermarket Sweep on page 111. Use stuffed animals and small, realistic-looking hardened rubber animals from a home or classroom toy chest to set the theme for another Move and Match game called Going to the Zoo on page 113. A plastic playhouse can be used in the Mitten Match activity in chapter 9 (page 117) and as a building in the village in the cycling lessons in chapter 10 (page 138). Remember: When funds are limited, look first to what you already have on hand.

Making Equipment

Next, let's consider how you might make your own equipment from inexpensive materials you may already have around the house or purchase for little cost at a hardware or discount store. Walking Blocks and Lucy the Whale, in chapters 4 and 12, respectively, are two examples of homemade equipment. Ask others to help if you do not have the tools, skills, or time for these and other equipment construction projects. Consider recruiting parent volunteers to construct needed equipment. One approach is to ask interested parents to sign up when they are visiting your program at an autumn open house. You could also ask a junior high school technology education teacher to have students construct equipment such as walking blocks as a project. One word of caution: Check with your program administrator to determine whether there is a policy that prohibits the use of homemade and donated equipment in your movement program.

We recommend making theme cards to use in many of the activities in this book (see figure 2.1), especially the Move and Match activities in chapter 9 and the cycling and fitness and nutrition activities in chapters 10 and 11, respectively. Theme cards are made from 8 1/2-inch by 11-inch card stock cut in half with a picture and word on each card. They can also be made from colored construction paper and cut in various shapes, then laminated for durability. Make at least five theme cards for every child, or 50 to 75 cards for a class of 18 children. Theme cards are simple to make, but they take time. Investigate whether there is a library of pattern-making dies available to you. These dies cut multiple copies of the same shape (circle, square, bat, rabbit, or many other shapes) in just a few seconds. Using these dies really saves time when you need to make many copies of a single shape. Perhaps dies are available for your use at a nearby teacher center or instructional materials center. Failing that, ask if a parent would volunteer to cut and laminate the shapes.

Distribute the work so that you or a volunteer make one new set of theme cards each month. Over the span of a year, you will have several sets of theme cards for your movement program. Over several years, you will have constructed and accumulated a rich and diverse collection of theme cards ready for use on a moment's notice in a variety of movement program activities.

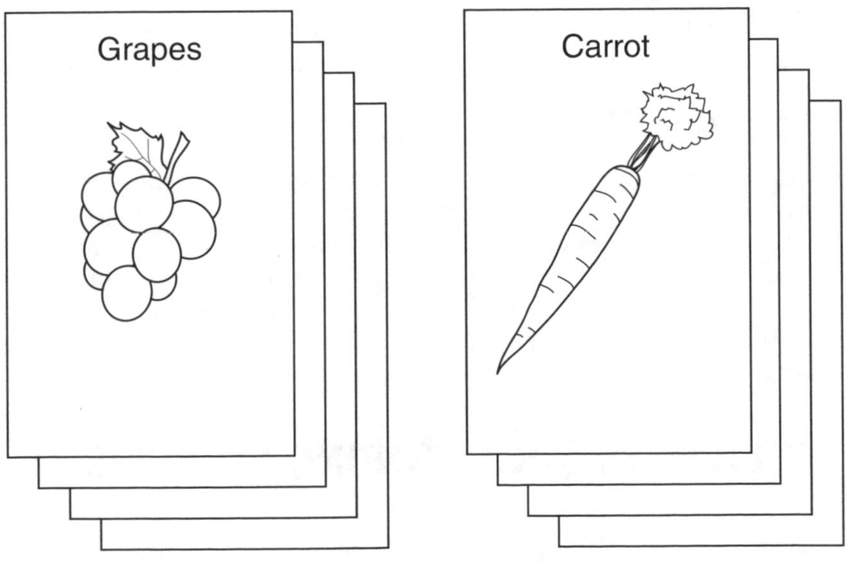

Figure 2.1 An example of theme cards used in a movement program.

Requesting Donations

Before heading to a store to buy needed equipment for a movement activity, ask whether people you know have a surplus of such equipment or materials to donate. Many people have perfectly useable items that they no longer want piled in their attics, basements, garages, or storage rooms. Get the word out to family, friends, colleagues, and children's parents when you are in need of equipment. Plastic roller skates, wooden ladders, sheets, balls, toys, and stuffed animals are just a few of the many items people may be happy to donate.

Learn about the children's parents' employment with an eye toward requesting donations of surplus materials from their jobs for use in your program. One parent worked for a large overnight shipping company and, upon learning that bubble wrap was used in movement activities in chapter 4, arranged the donation of several enormous rolls of bubble wrap. Another parent worked in construction and donated surplus lengths of gutters ideal for the gutter games in chapter 8.

Request donations of funds for the purchase of large, expensive equipment that you cannot make. Ask the local county health department and American Heart Association to donate curriculum kits and materials that teach fitness and nutrition concepts, as discussed in chapter 11. Approach local civic organizations for funds to purchase bicycles, bike helmets, Lucy the whale, and other more expensive items that clearly benefit young children. The parent–teacher organization may be a source of funds if you conduct a movement program in a school setting. Be sure to thank publicly each organization that makes a donation to your program.

Shopping at Discount Stores

You can have great success discovering inexpensive materials to use creatively in movement activities at discount department stores or dollar stores. Many of the activities in this book use materials and equipment that can be purchased very inexpensively in these discount stores. Remember to also check thrift stores for toys, skates, holiday decorations, and other items that are still serviceable and can be purchased for a fraction of their original price.

SETTING UP AND STORING EQUIPMENT

Movement programs are commonly conducted in spaces that are used for multiple purposes, requiring that all equipment be taken down and stored at the end of the class and put up again the next day. Renée McCall faces this same task every day. We offer time-saving ideas in this section that can make setting up and storing equipment as easy as possible.

Tying and untying ropes can make the setup and takedown of equipment such as nets very time consuming. We recommend using such things as bolt snaps, bungee cords, and duct tape to eliminate the need to tie and untie ropes. In chapter 5 we explain how to secure eyebolts in opposing walls (at three heights—low, waist height, and high overhead) and then attach bolt snaps to each end of a rope and stretch it taut across the open space. Clip the bolt snaps onto the eyebolts to firmly anchor the rope. Now you can use the rope for a net (waist high) or scooter pull (low), or as a support for a pulley activity (overhead). Once you have the ropes attached to the eyebolts using bolt snaps, do not untie the ropes. Instead, unsnap the ropes, coil them, and store them in a labeled baggie. Have ropes dedicated for each use so you never have to measure and cut each rope more than once. This makes setting up for activities with ropes and eyebolts super simple because all you have to do the next time is uncoil the rope and snap it onto the eyebolts.

Use bungee cords to save time anchoring ropes to supports such as trees, basketball supports, or other anchors for which eyebolts are not practical. Wrap the bungee cord tightly around the support, then clip the bolt snap over the tightly wound bungee cord to anchor the rope. Takedown is also quick because there are no knots to undo.

Use duct tape to adhere laminated theme cards to large poster characters, described in the Move and Match activities in chapter 9. Duct tape, unlike masking tape, can be adhered to and removed from a wall or other surface many times over and will still stick. Just remove the duct tape before storing the theme cards in a clearly labeled envelop; then store them in a file cabinet until the next time you need them. Also use duct tape to hold lightweight objects in place, such as the pulleys on the overhead rope described in the Go Fish activity in chapter 5. Store the duct tape on the rope so you don't need to reassemble it the next time you play the activity.

Supervision is key for safety. Any piece of equipment can become dangerous if used without adult supervision. Every activity in this book is designed to be conducted under attentive adult supervision.

RESOURCES

Please note that catalog stock changes from year to year. Visit several of the Web sites to ascertain product availability or call to request a current equipment catalog.

- Constructive Playthings at www.cptoys.com, phone 1-800-448-1412
- FlagHouse at www.flaghouse.com, phone 1-800-793-7900

- Gopher at www.gophersport.com, phone 1-800-533-0446
- Omnikin at www.omnikin.com, phone 1-800-706-6645
- Play With a Purpose at www.playwithapurpose.com, phone 1-800-533-0446
- Sportime at www.sportime.com, phone 1-800-444-5700
- US Games at www.us-games.com, phone 1-800-327-0484. The US Games preschool and elementary physical education catalog is titled Learning Through Movement.

chapter 3

Music, Please!

Toya really likes the movement activities that she conducts each day in her class. Today, the children enjoyed each movement experience, yet Toya sensed that the movement experiences seemed somehow sterile, as if they were missing something. As she clapped her hands to help a child jump rhythmically, she had an insight. What if she could find jut the right music to accompany each movement! If she could, the children's enthusiasm for movement would probably increase. Moreover, enthusiastic children are happier and seem to learn more quickly. Yes, music could make her movement activities better, but some questions came to Toya's mind:

- How would she know which music best matches with each activity?
- What styles of music would motivate children?
- Where would she find music with appropriate lyrics for children?

THIS CHAPTER OFFERS Toya and others many suggestions for selecting and using appropriate music with movement activities. It discusses what effect music has on young children and how it can be used to facilitate learning and enjoyment. It gives suggestions for involving children in music by using simple instruments to make rhythms, following dictated instructions with musical accompaniment, and using music for motivation in movement activities. Many specific music collections and selections, including catalogs that carry music titles suitable for young children, are referenced for your convenience (also see the "Resources" section at the end of chapter 2 on page 23).

We recommend that music be an integral part of a movement curriculum for young children. We strongly encourage the use of music when teaching movement for children for several reasons. According to music researcher Sally Moomaw, music encourages a variety of physical knowledge and a deeper understanding of our bodies and how we make ourselves move (Moomaw 1997). These are important concepts for developing children. Moomaw reported the following:

- Music assists in the development of skillful movement.
- Music helps children develop motor skills and body awareness.
- Music accompanying movement helps children develop coordination and encourages imagination.

In addition, some research indicates that music aids cognitive development. It helps children think better. Neurological research indicates that exposure to music heightens children's cognitive development by helping them develop complex reasoning skills (Moomaw, 1997). Most important, music provides children with emotional release because it offers a way for them to express what they are feeling in a safe and socially acceptable way. Music can free young children, who still have limited vocabularies, from the need to "use their words" to express their feelings. Musical cues such as rhythm, tempo, instrumentation, volume, texture, form, timbre, pitch, and melodic and harmonic structure give children many opportunities to express and work through emotions such as joy, frustration, fear, and sadness.

Moving to a musical beat allows children to freely and happily express themselves.

Music can be an integral part of movement lessons for young children. Begin selecting music with some general considerations in mind. Rae Pica, an expert on music and movement, provides guidelines for selecting music to accompany a movement lesson. Select music with a clear, simple rhythm and distinctive instrumentation. Children need to be able to hear the rhythm easily if they are to move to it. Be sure that any lyrics are easy to understand if you ask children to respond to the words. "Variety not only helps maintain interest, but also familiarizes students with musical elements—and movement—they might not otherwise experience" (Pica 1999, 33).

With these general guidelines in mind, let's consider how to select music that will support movement activities. You can use music to help children develop a sense of rhythm, learn to follow instructions (through dictated movement songs), and learn locomotor skills (by playing music that matches the skill's rhythm). Music can also provide structure to the movement lesson, alter moods by stimulating or calming children, and stimulate movement exploration. Let's consider each of these six uses of music on the following pages.

DEVELOPING A SENSE OF RHYTHM

Use music to enable children to develop a sense of rhythm and keep a steady beat. This is important because rhythm underlies all movement. Remember that music does not always need instrumentation. One ancient use of music is easy to implement. You need only your voice and the voices of children chanting. Chants are a great way to develop a sense of rhythm through clapping, stomping, tapping, or stepping in time to the music you sing. Children love to sing and love to move. What a combination! Chants are quick and easy to organize, and they involve no equipment and little space. They are also a simple way to use music if you don't have a library of music and a CD player. You can do a chant on the spot, whether indoors or outdoors. Just gather the children and start to sing and swing.

A large variety of preschool instructional books are available with chants and songs for circle time. One well-established resource with a variety of chants exploring gross motor movement is the *Piggyback Songs* series. The songbooks are available through Kimbo Educational at www.kimboed.com on CD and cassette as well as in print, so an instructor can learn the tunes or sing along with the balladeer. You may also want to expand beyond chants by adding rhythm instruments. A variety of rhythm instruments that are homemade, donated from home, or purchased inexpensively can provide a perfect way to learn rhythm, tempo, and pitch.

- Create rhythm sticks for children to beat together or on the floor, using a foot-long dowel or tightly rolled paper. Let them experience the different sounds of wood versus rolled paper striking the floor.
- Make wrist bells by sewing jingle bells on elastic strips.
- Create maracas by sealing rice inside snack-size cereal boxes.
- Create a drum from a can with a plastic lid or a pot turned upside down.
- Purchase a large assortment of play instruments for children, including recorders, tambourines, drums, and harmonicas at a dollar store.
- Have the children walk, march, or simply bend their knees while beating out 3/4 and 4/4 time.

Another excellent way to reinforce children's sense of rhythm is to have them listen to a metronome or rhythm machine for a minute before starting their warm-up. Rhythm machines are electronic devices that can be set to produce a variety of rhythms at various tempos, pitches, and tone qualities. They are available from music stores. Using rhythm will help organize children's bodies directly before the musical warm-up that follows. Ask children to clap or stomp along with a chosen rhythm. Let's say the warm-up song you select is set in 4/4 time. Set the rhythm machine to a fun rhythm that is in 4/4 time, such as a mambo. Ask children to move their bodies to the beat, whether they swing their arms, bend their knees, or twist their waist as they attempt to match the beat with their movements. To aid them in getting the beat, accentuate the beat with your own body movements and lead children in the chant "We've got the beat. We've got the beat. We've got the beat . . ." Once this internal beat is established, immediately begin the warm-up with the dictated music in 4/4 time such as in the song "The Body Rock " on the Greg & Steve *Kids in Motion* CD. This approach can be helpful to children in establishing rhythmicity and organizing their movements. If you are also asking children to sing along as they move, Phyllis Weikert recommends first establishing the song's anchor pitch. This is the pitch of the first note of the song, introduced by the adult singing a two-measure introduction on the first note's pitch, using words such as "One, two, ready, sing" (Weikert 1997, 2). Refer to the work of Phyllis Weikert (available through High/Scope Educational Research Foundation in Ypsilanti, Michigan) for a further discussion of developing rhythm and movement.

Before concluding this discussion of chants, we want to share a favorite singing chant of ours. You may want to use it at the end of each lesson to help children transition from the movement lesson to the next part of their day. We find that behavior difficulties are most likely to occur during transitions from one activity to the next. Children may handle the transition better when you avoid saying, "Now class is over," and instead focus on what you will do the next time in the movement lesson when you meet. Following an established routine for the final minutes of every class can be very helpful. Preschool children may enjoy singing this short song:

"So long, we'll see you tomorrow.
So long, we'll see you tomorrow.
So long, we'll see you tomorrow.
Please have a happy day."

This song is a cheery, positive way to end the lesson. If you don't already have a favorite way of closing your movement lesson, we hope you will try this song to the tune of any of your favorite songs.

LEARNING TO FOLLOW INSTRUCTIONS

Use music to help children learn to follow instructions through dictated movement songs. These songs have verbal instructions or cues on how to move within the context of the song itself. The singer typically challenges children to identify body parts or perform motor skills. Some songs have children bending, twisting, and turning in place, whereas other tunes have these young movers galloping, jumping, and walking backward. These activities can be performed in small or large spaces, depending on the movements that are requested. Dictated movement songs are often available in either CD or audiocassette format. Here are some CDs that contain dictated movement songs popular with children. We've placed a favorite song on each CD in parentheses or in the text.

- Peter and Ellen Allard's *Sing It! Say It! Stamp It! Sway It! Vol. 2* (with our favorite song, "Bodies 1-2-3") is a CD that we highly recommend because children love it. The CD contains locomotor movement songs, circle time songs, and finger plays, although the latter would not be used for gross motor movement lessons. It also contains energetic songs suitable as background music during movement activities. The CD is available at www.PeterandEllen.com with lyrics that can also be printed in a printer-friendly format from the Web site.
- The *Greg & Steve* series is another favorite with children. Their songs explore locomotor and nonlocomotor movement, body identification, and spatial awareness as well as uses of beanbags. The songs have current, motivating tunes that stimulate children to move.

Consider starting with the CD *Kids in Action* (with our favorite song, "Can't Sit Still"), *Kids in Motion* (with the song "The Body Rock"), or *On the Move* (and with favorite song "Warmin' Up [1]"). The CD is produced by Youngheart Records and available through the Greg & Steve Web site at www.gregandsteve.com.

- The Learning Station CDs *Tony Chestnut & Fun Time Action Songs* (with its lively action songs and circle games), and *Physical Ed* (a fun fitness music video and CD), are both excellent for promoting movement and locomotor activities. Children also enjoy their music video *Movin' & Groovin'*. These resources are available on the Web at www.learningstationmusic.com.
- Jeffrey Friedberg currently has two energizing CDs that are smash hits with children. *Snortin' Norton's Car Trip* has the perfect combination song for working on locomotor skills. The song "Green Light Go" is a fun way to learn the concept of stop and go. Other songs teach locomotor movements, finger plays, and sing-alongs. There is also a great song about senses titled "Something Smells." Friedberg's *Bossy Frog* CD (with the lead song "Bossy Frog") is also a crowd-pleaser that has children jumping, swinging, hopping, and dancing. These two CDs are available at www.amazon.com.
- Kimbo Educational offers three CD favorites titled *Preschool Action Time* (with our favorite song "Play Days"), *Preschool Aerobic Fun* (with the song "Slow Stretching"), and the *Action Songs for Preschoolers* (with the song "Bendable, Stretchable"). These CDs offer fun locomotor and nonlocomotor activity songs, body part identification, and spatial awareness exercises along with finger plays. These are classic, high-quality movement songs that children love. Two other crowd pleasers from Kimbo Records contain songs that use beanbags and address coordination skills. *Bean Bag Activities* (with our favorite song "Bean Bag Rock") and *Bean Bag Fun* (with the song "On the March") are both helpful when teaching body identification, rhythm, and balance. Most of these CDs are available from Kimbo Educational at www.kimboed.com.
- Activity Records' classic *Children's All-Star Rhythm Hits* CD by Jack Capon and Rosemary Hallum contains many wonderful songs for movement. Two of the ever-popular Hap Palmer series *Walter the Waltzing Worm* (with the song "What a Miracle") and *Sally the Swinging Snake* (with the song "Wiggy Wiggy Wiggles") also contain activity songs involving locomotor and nonlocomotor skills, body part identification, and spatial awareness. These three CDs are all available on the Educational Activities Web site at www.edact.com. Just search using the singers' names. They are also available through the Constructive Playthings catalog.

- *Dragon Tales: Dragon Tunes* CD (with our favorite "Wiggle Song") facilitates children's movements by encouraging them to imitate dragons. Children dance through a magical dragon land. This CD is available through www.kidrhino.com/kids25.htm.
- Walt Disney Music Company has several CDs for movement activities. We recommend *Living La Vida Mickey* and Dance Party Favorites, and any of the more than 20 CDs and cassettes featuring dance party music, dictated movements, and Mickey singing popular songs suitable for young children at www.disney.go.com/DisneyRecords/Kids.html. If you want children to experience one of the most stimulating versions of the Hokey Pokey out today, try the CD titled *Little Richard: Shake It All About* produced by the Disney Music Company and available at www.amazon.com.
- *Wiggles: Dance Party* CD (and the song "Can You [Point Your Fingers and Do the Twist?]"), by the Australian group the Wiggles, features a variety of action songs along with wacky, funky interludes between songs that children find entertaining. This CD is available through www.amazon.com. Other CDs by the Wiggles are available at their Web site http://shop.thewiggles.com.au/.

LEARNING LOCOMOTOR SKILLS

Use music to help children learn to perform locomotor skills at a steady tempo by mindfully selecting and playing music that has the same meter, rhythm, and tempo as the skill you want them to practice (refer to "Music Terms" on this page for definitions of these terms).

If you want children to learn to gallop or slide, select music with a quick tempo in common time (4/4). Pica (1999) encourages teachers to use varied musical selections to help children differentiate between sustained and suspended movements and between step-hop and skip-

Music Terms

- The meter is the "pattern created by accented and unaccented beats, or how beats are grouped together."
- The rhythm is the "patterns made by the length and accents of sounds."
- The tempo is the "speed music moves at and an important element of its physiological effect. Steady tempos can be measured in beats per minute."

From Miles 1997, 252.

ping movements. She notes that playing music with a galloping rhythm lets children hear the rhythm of this motor skill. The song "Betcha Can" from the *Dragon Tales: Dragon Tunes* CD is a good example of dictated music to accompany children as they learn to jump and hop. The song "Gallop" on the *Physical Ed* CD by the Learning Station is a fun way to practice galloping to a strolling rhythm of a horse on a trail ride. This CD is available at www.amazon.com. The *Motion Series*, initially created for people rehabilitating from traumatic brain injuries, can also help all young children develop rhythmic gait (walking) patterns, according to the company Mayatek. The CD consists of pleasant melodies that are layered over a consistent beat. We particularly enjoy volume one, track four (there are no titles for these tracks). The CD insert explains,

> Children and adults with normal hearing respond rapidly and predictably to musical input. In many common forms of neurological injury the primary auditory area of the brain is spared, which controls movement to music. The "dancing brain" controls movement to music and can orchestrate complex movements despite severe damage to the primary motor areas. The *Motion Series* has been composed and arranged to encourage gross motor movements. (*Motion Series* CD jacket 2001)

To purchase the CD, write to Mayatek at P.O. Box 15640, Fort Worth, TX 76119, or call 817-572-0009.

PROVIDING STRUCTURE

Another effective way to use music is as background sound to provide structure to each movement lesson. Teach children that when the music starts, it is time to begin moving. When it stops, it is time to freeze and listen for instructions. This common, easy way of signaling for attention is enjoyable to children and will save your voice. The use of music to signal for attention is preferable to the ever-present whistle used by physical education teachers decades ago. It also eliminates the need to raise your voice to be heard over active children. Teach children to listen to and respond to the music cues through playing games in which children start and stop with the music cue. Consider playing a simple version of Stop and Go to Music as explained in McCall and Craft (2000, 120-121). Time spent early in the year teaching children to start and stop in response to musical cues is well worth the effort.

If you already use music in your program, you may feel tethered to the music source, unable to roam the room to instruct an individual child because you need to be next to the sound system to turn the music on and off. If your budget allows, purchase a sound system that has a remote control. Carry the remote in your pocket while teaching so that you can turn the music on and off from anywhere in the room.

The type of music you play will influence the mood of the children. Consider the mood you want to create when selecting the music you intend to play as background for giving structure to your movement lessons. We list several suggestions in the following section.

ALTERING MOODS

Use stimulating or calming music to alter children's moods. Many people become energized when they listen to upbeat music. When listening to music with a slower tempo (fewer cycles per second), most people tend to become more relaxed. Music in major and minor keys also has different effects on listeners' moods. Pica reminds us that "whether you need to bring peace to overstimulated children, make routine activities more enjoyable, or provide a little extra energy at a low point in the day, music is the key" (1999, 32).

Following is a teacher-tested and child-approved list of suggested music to alter moods. We hope it will be useful whether you are just developing a musical library or expanding an established one.

Energizing and Stimulating Music

Select energizing and stimulating music if you want children to exercise vigorously. For example, play lively music in the background if you want to keep children stimulated and motivated as they cycle continuously for several minutes, developing their cardiovascular endurance. The following musical selections provide energizing background music with a steady beat for use while children warm up or practice skills, or anytime children need a burst of energy. We've included our favorite selection from each CD in the text or in parentheses after the CD title.

- Sugar Beats has a series of CDs with great rhythm, tempo, and beat. The songs are new and old chart toppers, sung by children, and compiled by Razor & Tie Direct. The *Back to the Beat* CD with the song "Loco-Motion" is great. The CD is available through www.amazon.com.
- *Kidz Bop* is another series of CDs of popular music played regularly on the radio. Many children will surely recognize these tunes. We especially enjoy the selections "All Star" and "Livin' la Vida Loca" on the original *Kidz Bop* CD. These songs, sung by children to various adult accompaniment, are also available through www.amazon.com.
- The *ESPN Presents: Jock Jams* series are energetic, stimulating compilations of sports arena music that children will bop to from start to finish. We particularly recommend *ESPN Presents: Jock Jams, Volume*

4 (with our favorite song "Space Jam"). These CDs are available through Tommy Boy Music at www.amazon.com.

- The *For Our Children* series offers popular artists singing classic and original children's songs. "This Old Man" sung by Bob Dylan is especially good. *Minnie 'n Me* is another favorite that features a young teenager singing cute songs with a clear beat. These are just two of several CDs produced by the Walt Disney Music Company that are ideal for background music or accompaniment for exercise routines. These CDs are available from www.amazon.com.
- The many Putumayo CDs offer wonderful songs from a variety of cultures and musical traditions. We especially enjoy the CD *Putumayo Presents: World Playground* (and the song "Boom, Boom Tarara"). These CDs are available through Putumayo World Music (www.putumayo.com).
- *Reggae for Kids*, including our favorite song "Reggae Rock" by Michigan and Smiley, is available through RAS Records (www.rasrecords.com). This CD and others by these artists enable children to experience culturally diverse music with varying tempos and rhythms.

Calming and Soothing Music

The following musical selections contain calming background music useful in helping children relax. Play any of these selections as an accompaniment during the cool-down after vigorous physical activity, during a quiet time in the classroom, or anytime children become too stimulated and need a soothing sound.

- The *Tune Your Brain* CD, especially *Tune Your Brain With Mozart: Focus,* is helpful in positively influencing mood. The CD is consistent with the writings by Elizabeth Miles about music's influence on the brain. The CD is available on the Web at www.tuneyourbrain.com.
- Baby Einstein also has a series of classical music CDs. We find that children especially enjoy the very famous "Für Elise" by Beethoven on the *Baby Einstein* CD. These CDs are created for infants, but are also appropriate for young children. According to the CD jacket, "Studies have shown a relationship between listening to classical music and the development of spatial intelligence, reasoning, and other cognitive skills." (*Baby Einstein* 2002) Along with *Baby Einstein*, enjoy *Baby Mozart*, *Baby Bach*, and *Baby Vivaldi*. Visit www.babyeinstein.com.
- Enya's CD *Paint the Sky With Stars* (and her song "Book of Days") is soothing music that helps relax anxious bodies. Enya's music is available through Warner Music at www.warnermusic.co.uk.

- Kevin Roth's *Dinosaurs & Dragons* is specifically geared to young listeners. This CD has a wonderful blend of classic sing-alongs and peaceful melodies. We especially enjoy the song "Dragon, Dragon." The CD is available through Kiddo Music at www.kiddomusic.com/RothKevin.html.

STIMULATING MOVEMENT EXPLORATION

Use music to stimulate slow movement exploration in each child's personal space as well as to enable each child to make his or her own movement choices. If you want children to develop self-expression and creative movement, forego the dictated music and use classical music from the *Baby Einstein* CD as a background to prompt such creativity.

Music can also stimulate the opportunity for children to create their own movement activities or exercise routines. Put on music that has a steady rhythm and an upbeat tempo. *Kidz Bop* (with the song "All Star") and *ESPN Presents: Jock Jams* (and the song "Space Jam") are just two of the many possibilities from the music suggested earlier in this chapter. Let children decide what body part they want to warm up or what locomotor movement they want to perform. Ask the group as a whole what body part they want to warm up, and someone is likely to give a suggestion. Young children may occasionally need you to give a choice to get them started. Coach younger children by asking, "Do you want to choose your leg or your arm?" As children state their choices, give it a try and then move on to the next suggestion. By giving children the opportunity to make decisions in what they will be doing, you enable them to be stakeholders in the activity. Refer to "Resources" at the end of chapter 2 on page 23 for several companies that publish equipment and supply catalogs for teaching movement and sports. These catalogs contain some of the musical selections we've highlighted in this chapter along with other favorites. The catalogs for Constructive Playthings and Play With a Purpose are the only two that focus exclusively on equipment and instructional materials for young learners. Other companies listed in chapter 2 designate early childhood sections within their general catalogs. Look for music under the following sections: rhythms, preschool music, or music and movement.

In part II of this book you will learn motivating movement activities that use a variety of novel, inexpensive equipment. Combine these activities with music for fun, exciting movement lessons.

Part II

Activities for Purposeful Play

The movement activities in part II are the heart and soul of this book. These activities are organized into six chapters based on the type of inexpensive equipment they require. Each of these activities is teacher tested and child approved, having been used successfully in movement programs for young children. We present them in an easy-to-read format that includes equipment tips, adaptations for children with special needs, and variations to change the challenge level. In this section you will learn how to use inexpensive equipment in novel ways to stimulate joy and purpose in children's movement!

chapter 4

Inexpensive Starter Activities

Ms. Barry just returned from a great workshop on conducting movement programs for young children. She wants to begin offering a movement program right away, but knows that it will take months before she can purchase any equipment through the official channels. She is excited enough about beginning a movement program that she is willing to spend her own money for equipment to get started, but she doesn't want to go overboard and make expensive purchases.

In this chapter you will find seven activities that can get you started at very little expense. Both teachers and young children will love these starter activities. Young children will love them because they are fun to play. Teachers will love them because they teach movement skills using equipment that is inexpensive, easy to assemble, and easy to transport. This makes the activities easy to play on the spur of the moment almost anywhere.

Each of the following activities helps children develop different skills and uses different equipment, yet any one activity can be played using equipment that can be obtained for under $5.00. Read on for ideas that can get your movement program started.

Roll Out the Bubble Wrap

Locomotor skills • Cardiovascular endurance

Roll out the bubble wrap, then hop and pop. Children can get a great cardiovascular workout as they play nonstop on bubble wrap—walking, jumping, crawling, and hopping with glee just to hear those bubbles pop. Bubble wrap is easy to set up and

works well in very small to large spaces. If you think that you can monitor it safely, have children play in bare feet to increase the sensory stimulation. One young child with Down syndrome had learned to walk, but was reluctant to run. When placed on strips of bubble wrap taped to the floor, however, he gleefully ran, and ran, and ran, delighting in the sound of popping bubbles.

Overview

With shoes and socks on or off, children use a variety of locomotor skills to move across the bubble wrap taped to the floor.

Goals for Children

- Develop locomotor skills
- Develop additional movement concepts such as the bear walk and the roll
- Experience sensory stimulation when played in bare feet

Equipment

- Sheets of bubble wrap with small bubbles
- Clear packing tape or duct tape
- CD of lively music
- CD player

Equipment Tips

Purchase a roll of bubble wrap at the dollar store or from an office supply store. A local dollar store charges $1 for a five-foot length (2 m) of bubble wrap. Request donations from businesses that use large quantities of bubble wrap. Save it from packages you and friends receive. Poll parents of the children in your program to learn if any of them has access to free bubble wrap. One parent who works for an express mail company arranged for the donation of several years' supply of bubble wrap to a movement program.

Preparation

Spread the bubble wrap on the floor. For safety, secure the wrap in place with clear or duct tape so that it will not shift as the children run and jump on it.

Instructions

1. Have the children sit and remove their shoes and socks, if you wish.
2. Encourage the children to experiment with stepping on the bubble wrap to hear the pops as their weight bursts individual bubbles.
3. Turn on lively music and let the children move across the bubble wrap in whatever safe manner and direction they wish. Some may move quickly along the length of the wrap. Others may jump in place.
4. As the children are moving about, encourage each child to move in a more challenging way. Encourage children who move slowly to move faster. Encourage children who are jumping but landing unevenly to land on two feet simultaneously. Encourage children who are crawling to do a bear walk, using only their hands and feet rather than crawling on their knees.

Adaptations

Nonambulatory children may roll or creep (pulling with their arms and pushing with their legs while moving on their bellies) on the bubble wrap, popping the bubbles with their hands or body. Place a child who may not be able to roll or crawl in adapted equipment, such as the mobile prone stander shown in figure 1.1a on page 10 in chapter 1. The wheels will pop the bubbles as the child moves.

Some children have severe pica tendencies (that is, they try to eat or chew nonedible objects). Consider placing children who are likely to put their mouths on the bubble wrap in gait trainers. This lets them walk on the wrap, but prevents them from bending over and putting their mouths on it.

Variations

- Start the activity by giving the children who appear a bit apprehensive the opportunity to simply stand in bare feet on the wrap.
- Use the bubble wrap, along with a variety of equipment, as part of an obstacle course. Involve several locomotor tasks such as crawling on equipment, as well as walking or galloping on the bubble wrap.

Changing the Space

- In a small space, cover the entire floor with the bubble wrap and let the children explore moving.
- In a large space, you may wish to cover the entire area with bubble wrap or simply place a long strip of the wrap on the floor to create a path along which the children move.

- Using bubble wrap outdoors on a sidewalk or driveway is unsafe because of the abrasive, hard surface of blacktop or cement. The activity could be done on a softer, grassy area, with the children wearing shoes, but the bubbles will not pop easily.

Bubble Wrap Mail Delivery

Motor planning • Locomotor skills

Object, color, and shape recognition • Spatial relationships

Create a movement path along which children perform a variety of locomotor skills as they collect and deliver mail and peel and place stickers. This activity is excellent for sensory input as children walk barefoot on the bubble wrap and handle stickers with their fingers. The instructions use the theme of mailing valentines here, but the themes can be limitless.

Overview

Lay down the bubble wrap to create a large square movement path on the floor. Ask the children to move along each side of the square. At each corner add a task for the children to do that sends them to the next corner. As an example, create an activity around the children pretending to mail valentines.

Goals for Children

- Develop locomotor skills
- Use a pincer grasp
- Perform tasks in sequence

Equipment

- Four sheets of at least 2-foot-wide bubble wrap (1 m); to create a path that forms a 25-foot square, use four 25-foot lengths of bubble wrap (8 m)
- Playhouse, climber, stands, or other props, one at each corner
- Paper valentines, laminated for durability
- Valentine stickers

Equipment Tips

Short paths can be created with very inexpensive five-foot sheets of bubble wrap purchased at a dollar store, a hardware store, or an office supply store.

Preparation

Tape strips of bubble wrap in a shape of a large square on the floor. Tape four strips of bubble wrap onto the floor at right angles to each other, to make a path that forms a square, with no bubble wrap in the center.

Instructions

1. Begin the activity by asking each child to take a sticker off the sheet of stickers, thereby practicing the pincer grasp.
2. The children move along the bubble wrap path, walking, jumping, or however you suggest or they decide to move, to the first corner. Here there is a large paper valentine posted on the wall or displayed on a table. Children are to stick their stickers on the large valentine.
3. Next, the children move to the second corner, where they each get a small paper valentine.
4. Then the children move along the bubble wrap to the third corner where there is a post office made from a large box, overturned laundry baskets, plastic playhouse, or whatever is available. Here the children pretend to mail their small paper valentines. If it does not disrupt the flow of the activity, ask children to say the names of the objects pictured on the cards as they hand them to you.
5. From here they move back to the first corner and begin their journey again.

Adaptations

Refer to the adaptations under Roll Out the Bubble Wrap on page 41.

Variations

You can vary the theme each time you use this activity.

- Create a spring flower theme with garden flower stickers to place on top of stems in a large flowerpot. Mail flower cards.
- Create a healthy foods theme using food stickers to be placed on a large paper plate or in a food basket. Mail cards with pictures of healthy food on them.
- Create a farm animal theme using stickers of animals to be placed on a large paper picture of a barn yard. Mail cards with pictures of farm animals on them.
- Create a smiley face theme using smiley face stickers to be placed on a huge smiley face cut from yellow paper with a smiley face drawn on it. Mail cards with smiley faces on them.
- Use theme cards with letters or each child's name to further reinforce literacy skills.

Changing the Space

- In a small space with few children, use shorter and less expensive five-foot paths of bubble wrap for each side of the square. If the only available space is the end of an unused hallway, use two long strips of bubble wrap, joined by short connecting strips at either end, with stations placed along the way.
- In a large space, consider purchasing longer sheets for teaching many children.

Cheap Skate

Stability • Cardiovascular endurance • Motor planning

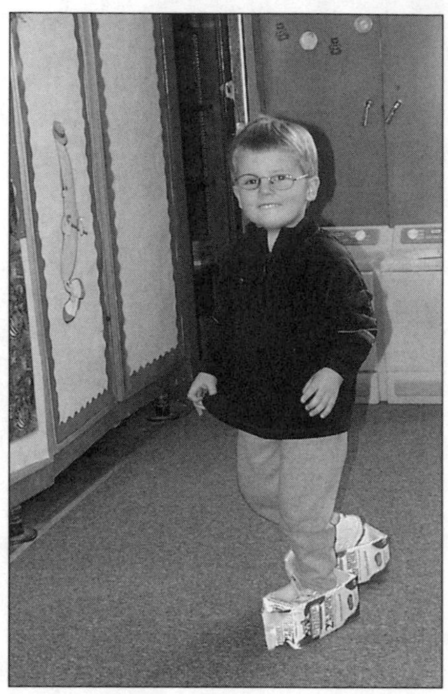

Whether or not the children are ready to experience their first set of ice skates, they will love to pretend they are skating. Practicing the reciprocal motions of skating will help them improve their coordination. Spring, summer, fall, or winter, here is a fun way to simulate skating that will have children imagining they are really on their own personal rink!

Overview

With shoes on, children can start skating by placing their feet in cut-out cardboard milk cartons. For children ready for an experience that is a bit more slippery, place old stockings over their shoes, and off they go.

Goals for Children

- Practice reciprocal arm and leg movements
- Increase cardiovascular endurance
- Practice stability

Equipment

- Half-gallon cardboard milk cartons (use pint cardboard milk cartons for very small feet)

- Nylon stockings
- Five props such as snowmen, paper trees, or whatever is at hand
- A portable playhouse, or large box, to serve as a warming hut
- CD, such as *Waldteufel: The Skaters' Waltz*
- CD player

Equipment Tips

Make pairs of skates from either milk cartons or stockings or both. Provide one pair per child. Cardboard milk cartons and stockings are free for the asking from neighbors, colleagues, relatives, and friends, or ask the children to bring in their own. Be sure you have a smooth, uncarpeted floor on which children can skate.

Preparation

Create a "real-life" skating atmosphere by adding a warming hut, made from a large box, a group of chairs, or a portable playhouse. The children can pretend to pick up their rental skates, rest, and warm up in the hut as needed. Decorate the skating area with paper trees supported in cones, large plastic snowmen bought on clearance, or other objects that can serve as props to add to the skating theme.

- Milk cartons: Cut out one side of a half-gallon milk or juice carton. For smaller feet, use a pint-size carton. Of course, make them by the pair.
- Stockings: Cut the foot section out of each stocking and knot the opening. This makes the toe area sturdier to withstand a child's pulling. Encourage the children's independence by asking them to slide the hose right over their sneakers. Depending on the length of the stocking, small stockings may just cover the shoe. With short stockings of only 5 to 8 inches (13 to 20 cm) in length, children can put the stockings over their shoes, similar to putting on a sock except that the sock goes on over the shoe. Longer stockings have enough extra length that the child can hold the other end of the stocking while skating and simulate the cross-country ski motion. With long stockings of 18 or more inches in length, children can slide the open end of the stocking over their shoes so that the long tail of the stocking hangs off the front of their shoes. Then they can hold the knotted end of the stocking in their hands. They now have a stocking extending from their hands to their feet. Pulling with their hands helps move their feet forward.

Instructions

1. Children can either stand or sit when stepping into the milk carton skates. It is best to have children sit when sliding on the stocking skates.
2. Once the skates are on, turn on music that fits the theme of a skating rink such as the CD titled *Waldteufel: The Skaters' Waltz,* produced by Nimbus Records and available through www.amazon.com. Encourage children to slide, twirl, and spin across the room as they pretend to skate on an ice rink.

3. As the children are skating, encourage them to skate forward, backward, fast with short strides, and slow with long strides. Remind children not to run in the skates.
4. Encourage children wearing the long stockings to use a reciprocating cross-country ski motion.

Adaptation

A child who is nonambulatory may wear the milk carton skates while using adapted equipment such as a gait trainer or a walker for support.

Variation

Children's plastic roller skates are also great to use when teaching beginners to roller-skate. Fun and stimulating ideas for roller skating can be found on page 110 in McCall and Craft (2000). Low-pile carpeted floors, such as those found in classrooms, are an excellent surface on which to begin learning to roller-skate. The carpet prevents the skates from rolling, giving children practice stepping on the skates. The carpet also cushions the children's falls.

Changing the Space

- In a small space, adjust the rink space accordingly for safe play.
- In a large space, expand the size of the rink and the obstacles presented to negotiate around.
- This activity will not work well outside because it requires a smooth, uncarpeted floor. When outdoors, switch to preschool-age roller skates, and, if your children are not ready for the driveway, head for the grass and have a safe, happy time!

Scoop It Up

Object control

Children love to play catch. Here is a quick and easy-to-create activity that allows even young children the opportunity to safely work on eye–hand coordination and experience success in both small and large spaces. The equipment is so easy to make that all children can have their own scoop and ball.

Overview

Using a ball scoop made from a plastic milk jug with a handle, children can practice catching a ball over and over and over again!

Goals for Children

- Develop eye–hand coordination

Equipment

- Plastic gallon jug
- Small, soft ball or one sheet of newspaper and masking tape to make a paper ball

Equipment Tip

This activity uses equipment commonly found around the house—plastic jugs, newspaper, and tape.

Preparation

Create a scoop by simply cutting the bottom out of a gallon plastic container. Tape the exposed edges to avoid scratches and cuts. Use a small, soft ball such as a foam ball, or make a ball by crumbling up newspaper and securing its round shape with masking tape.

Instructions

1. This activity works well as one of several stations in lessons on object control. Introduce the activity with a short demonstration. Instruct the children to hold the handle of the plastic container scoop in one hand, toss the ball in the air with the other hand, and then attempt to catch the ball in the scoop.
2. This is a problem-solving task. As the children practice, several will realize that if they do not toss the ball really high in the air, it will be easier to catch. You may want to assist other children in learning this concept. This skill is challenging and motivates children to keep trying it.

Adaptations

Children of all abilities can participate in this activity. Children with difficulty coordinating the catch and throw actions or with slow reaction times may do better when the ball is tossed to them from a short distance. They may also be more successful while seated, enabling them to prop the scoop in their laps for additional support with the handgrip.

Variations

- With more experienced children, use a smaller scoop and ball.
- Challenge one child to toss a ball underhand to another child who is holding the scoop. Have them vary the distance and height of the toss.
- Attach a string to the end of the scoop and tape it to the ball so that children can swing the ball up into the scoop. As with anything, activities with strings must be well supervised.

Changing the Space

In a small space, large space, or outdoors, simply accommodate as many children as the space safely allows.

Racquetball Fun With Hangers

Object control

This is a super-simple and inexpensive way to make rackets. Create a racket from a wire hanger and stocking in less than one minute! Easily make a racket for each child you teach. Children will enthusiastically and repeatedly use these rackets to practice striking, whether inside or outdoors.

Overview

Children delight in batting a cloth-covered balloon using a homemade racket. It is great fun to try to keep the balloon off the floor.

Goals for Children

- Develop eye–hand coordination

Equipment

One per child of the following, plus one roll of duct tape for everyone to use:

- One wire coat hanger
- One old nylon stocking
- A helium-quality balloon, covered with cloth for safety

- CD of lively music
- CD player

Equipment Tips

Need rackets? Stretch a hanger into a diamond, cover it with an old stocking, and wrap tape around the handle for a safe, inexpensive racket. Alternatively, make a racket from two paper dinner plates and a wooden paint stirrer.

Preparation

Create a flat racket from a wire coat hanger by stretching the hanger out so that it takes on a diamond shape. Slide an old stocking over the wire frame. Pull the stocking taut and tie the stocking in place so that it won't slide off. Squeeze the hook on the hanger top together to make a handhold. Wrap excess stocking around the handhold and then tape the wire to cover any sharp ends. There's your handle!

To make a racket from paper plates, tape the face of the two plates together to form the face of the racket. Then tape on a wooden paint stirrer to serve as the racket handle. This lightweight, but somewhat fragile, racket works well for striking cloth-covered balloons or paper balls, but not for heavier balls. (Thank you, Diana Boryk of the Yonkers Public Schools, Yonkers, New York, for this suggestion.)

Inflate a helium-quality balloon with air. Unlike regular balloons, helium-quality balloons are durable and do not break easily. For safety, cover the balloons in case they break. Place a piece of lightweight cloth over the balloon, and tie it together with string. Commercially made cloth coverings for balloons are called Balzacs.

Instructions

1. First discuss with the children the importance of looking before swinging the racket. With a child assisting, demonstrate at what distance it is safe to swing and when the space is too close. Children will need to wait or move to an open space before swinging.
2. Have the balloons nearby in a large container such as a box or large plastic bin.
3. After reviewing the instructions, turn on some lively music and release the balloons on to the floor for the children to pick up. Have the rackets close by so that the children may select their own.
4. Let the fun begin as the children repeatedly hit the balloons up in the air.

Adaptations

- Children of all abilities can participate in this activity. If children are unable to coordinate the use of rackets, encourage them to hit balloons in the air with their hands or have peers play catch with them, using balloons.
- Children's hands need to be free to do this activity. Prop children who are unable to stand so that they can sit and play this activity. Alternatively, place children who are unable to stand independently in mobile prone standers, gait

trainers, or similar adapted equipment that allows them to be upright without using their hands for support. For children unable to grasp the racket, simply toss a balloon to them so that they push it back using various body parts.

Variations

- Encourage children to count how many times they can hit their balloons in the air before they fall to the ground.
- Designate targets, such as cartoon characters, toward which the children must hit the balloon.
- Create a "tennis volley" by having two children hit a balloon back and forth to each other. Add a net!

Changing the Space

- In a small space, limit the number of children participating at one time. An alternative approach is to suspend the balloons from a rope or bar parallel to the floor and then have the children bat the balloons with their rackets in a more defined space.
- In a large space, or outdoors, let as many children participate as the space safely allows.

Walking Blocks

Stability • Spatial relationships

Small children love to imagine that they are part of a circus. Here's an easy way to create the dramatic play of a stilt walker, while working on balance, coordination, and spatial relationships.

Overview

With shoes on, children slip their feet through the ropes of a walking block and step, step, step. Add stickers for children to collect from props throughout the activity area, and everyone will have a fun time stilt walking.

Goals for Children

- Practice reciprocal movement of arms and legs
- Develop dynamic balance

Equipment

Each set of walking blocks requires the following:

- Two blocks of wood 4 1/2 inches (12 cm) long, cut from a two-by-four (50 mm × 100 mm, sanded framing or timber; or flatter and wider) length of lumber
- Two 24- to 36-inch (1 m) lengths of rope (taller children will require longer lengths)
- Two matching stickers for each pair of blocks (place one on each walking block to identify pairs of blocks)
- One sheet each of five different kinds of stickers, one for each of five props
- One card on a short string for each child
- CD of lively music
- CD player

Equipment Tips

Scour your garage or basement or ask parents and colleagues for suitable scrap wood from which to cut the blocks. Even if you must purchase the lumber from the local hardware store, it can be fairly inexpensive. Place a different sheet of stickers at each of the five props.

Preparation

Cut the wood to the suggested walking block dimensions. Drill a hole through the center of the width of each block. Feed the cut rope through the hole. Tie a knot, and you have a walking block (see figure 4.1). If the length of rope varies from one pair of blocks to the next, you will want to identify each pair of walking blocks so that children select blocks with identical lengths of rope. Use colorful, playful stickers to identify each pair of walking blocks. If you don't own a drill or a saw, ask a relative, neighbor, or industrial technology teacher at school to saw the blocks and drill the holes.

Place five or more props around the activity area. Then put a different sheet of stickers at each of the five props. Provide each child with a card on a string, worn as a bracelet, for collecting stickers.

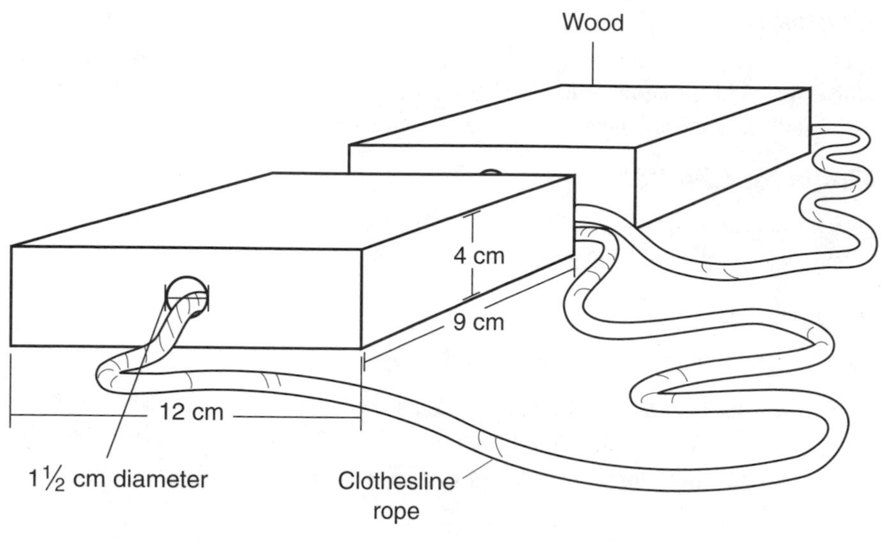

Figure 4.1 Walking block dimensions.

Instructions

1. Bring out the box or bin of walking blocks. As children reach for the walking blocks, encourage them to find matching pairs such as the matching stars, the matching bunnies, or the matching hearts.
2. Instruct children to place their feet on the blocks, pull up on the rope, and begin walking. It is essential to cue the children to pull up on the rope. Otherwise they will step right off the blocks as they start to move.
3. Instruct the children to walk to a specific destination or to stay within a designated area.
4. Add a task to the activity to maintain the children's focus and interest. Give each child a card to wear as a bracelet as he or she walks on the blocks. Challenge the children to walk around the five props placed throughout the activity area. At each prop, children are to peel off a sticker from the sheet of stickers at the prop and stick it on their own card.
5. Turn on some lively music, and let the stilt walking begin!
6. Use the collection of stickers to help children remain focused on the walking block activity. Positively redirect any children who might be wandering from the activity to find any stickers they have not yet collected. Conclude the activity when children have collected all five different stickers as they practice walking on the block "stilts."

Adaptations

Stilt walking may not be a suitable activity for children who are nonambulatory. Rather than exclude anyone, help these children practice mobility skills such as using a walker or braces for support, moving among their peers on the walking blocks. Paint the blocks bright colors for children who need practice with color discrimination.

Variations

- Choose thicker wood to increase the height of the walking block for more skilled children.
- Create an obstacle course for children to move through while on the walking blocks.
- Add gradual inclines and surface changes for children to walk across.
- Introduce a circus theme, and encourage the children to pretend they are walking on tall stilts. Play calliope music to reinforce the circus theme.

Changing the Space

- In a small space, reduce the number of children participating at one time.
- In a large space, add obstacles such as large plastic figurines of pumpkins, bunny rabbits—or just large decorated boxes— around which children are to negotiate.
- This activity works great outdoors. Children can walk on pavement or the grass. Let them move freely at their own pace or add obstacles to increase the challenge.

52 Pickup

Locomotor skills • Object control
Object, color, and shape recognition

You've heard the name; now let's play the game! Here's an incredibly easy way to motivate young children to move in a variety of ways, while at the same time creating a fun way to continue learning colors, shapes, and numbers.

Overview

Scatter plastic spoons, shapes, or playing cards all over the floor. Each child is given a particular object, such as a red spoon, and asked to find all the red spoons among the many colors of spoons scattered on the floor.

Goals for Children

- Develop grasping skill
- Develop dynamic balance as they stand, squat, and return to a stand
- Develop color recognition

Equipment

Use one dozen plastic spoons for each child who is playing. The following quantities are based on playing with four children. Scatter 10 of the 12 spoons of each color. Place one of the remaining two spoons in each child's bag at the beginning of the game to serve as a reminder of the color each child is seeking. Hold the other remaining spoon in your hand to show students if they pick up a mismatched spoon.

- 12 plastic green spoons
- 12 plastic blue spoons
- 12 plastic red spoons
- 12 plastic white spoons
- 4 bags or totes with handles (gift bags in colors that match spoon colors is an option)
- CD of lively music
- CD player

Equipment Tips

As an alternative, ask a local restaurant or retailer to donate white spoons. Send a request to families to send in spoons of a certain color. Plastic spoons are widely available at very inexpensive prices. Party stores typically have a large selection of colors.

If funds permit, use color-coordinated bags and plastic food, instead of spoons, for matching (available from Constructive Playthings at www.cptoys.com).

Preparation

This activity requires little preparation other than acquiring the spoons and bags and selecting an open space in which to play.

Instructions

1. Gather the children together. Explain that this is the place where they are to start and finish the game.
2. Ask the children to identify each of the colors to be used in the day's lesson. Then lead the children in counting aloud all the spoons of one color, so the children practice counting to 12 once. Consider providing a visual cue of each color and the numbers 1 to 12 on a large poster board.
3. Give each of the children a bag. Place a spoon of the color they are seeking in each of the children's bags so that they have a reminder of the color spoon they are seeking. Another approach is to tape an example of a spoon to the outside of the bag so children can more easily compare colors with the example on the bag. As stated earlier, an even better way is to purchase gift bags in colors that match the spoon colors. Give each child a bag that is the same color as the spoons the child is to collect. Now the child needs only to glance at the bag to be reminded of the color spoons to seek.
4. Explain that on the count of three you are going to throw all the spoons out onto the floor, but the children are to wait until they hear the music before they may start collecting the spoons.
5. Count to three and scatter the spoons. Start the music and let the children go!
6. Hold back one of each color spoon to use as a model. When a child mistakenly places an incorrectly matched spoon in the bag, ask the child to compare the correct color spoon, drawn from the extras in your hand, and the spoon the child just collected. Ask whether the two colors match. Repeat the color the child is to be seeking and have the child put the mismatched spoon back on the floor.
7. When all the spoons have been collected, stop the music and have the children return to the starting point.
8. Congratulate the children on a great job. Encourage them to tell each other "nice job." Begin the game again, switching the color each child is to find.

Adaptations

- Use adapted equipment such as a gait trainer or mobile prone stander to assist a child who is unable to walk independently. If a nonambulatory child is able to crawl, have all the children crawl as they gather the spoons. If needed, an adult can assist by placing the spoon in the child's hand and helping the child drop it into the bag.

- Also consider decreasing the number of spoons the child has to collect.
- Many young children with autism are proficient readers, so aid them in understanding the tasks by including the printed words as well as the pictures of each the colors on the poster board. Writing the printed word next to the picture also helps young readers.

Variations

When working with a small group of children, consider creating a poster board for each child—one for each color spoon collected—to reinforce the concept of numbers. Draw 12 rectangles with an outline of each of the 12 spoons with the corresponding numbers 1 through 12 under each rectangle. Place each poster board on a nearby table when doing this activity in a classroom. After the child collects the spoons, she or he then places one spoon over each of the 12 spoon outlines on the poster board for her or his spoon color. An additional variation is to attach Velcro to the back of each spoon and in each of the rectangles on the board. Now the spoons will remain secure within the rectangle, even if the child moves the poster boards. Here are some additional variations:

- Increase the number of spoons the children are to collect.
- Change the way the children are to move as they gather the spoons.
- Add a time limit to how long the children have to gather the spoons. Racing against time can be very motivating for young children. Always make sure the timer goes off after the last child has finished so that no one ever "loses."
- Add variety to what the children are to collect, such as having them collect six red and seven blue spoons.
- Have the children collect shapes such as squares, circles, or triangles instead of spoons.
- Use playing cards with advanced children. Challenge them to find all the threes, all the queens, cards of the same suit, or cards that total 21.
- Match colored bags with plastic foods of the same color.

Changing the Space

- In a small space, limit the number of children playing and the number of objects they must collect.
- In a large space, increase the number of children participating and the number of objects to be retrieved.
- This activity works really well outdoors. Children will be safest playing on grass, but the game can also be played on pavement.

chapter 5

Ropes, Pulleys, and Eyebolts

Tracy is a physical educator who travels between two schools. His schedule is such that he arrives at the school only five minutes before his kindergarten class is to begin. Right before his class, another physical educator is in the gymnasium teaching a fifth-grade class. They try to help each other, but it is difficult because the first teacher is usually so busy moving his equipment into the equipment room that he can't help Tracy with his setup. Tracy is continually searching for age-appropriate movement activities for young children that can be set up in the few minutes available to him.

TRACY'S SITUATION IS BY NO MEANS UNUSUAL for many teachers today. Large classes, tight schedules, and reduced budgets contribute to teachers' finding themselves teaching from the trunks of their cars. Movement teachers need to find ways to quickly set up and take down activity equipment without sacrificing class time or quality of activities. This chapter demonstrates how you can set up many motivating, appropriate activities quickly by using just a few simple pieces of ordinary hardware, such as eyebolts, permanently installed in the activity area.

A one-time installation of eyebolts in the walls of the activity area is a great way to set up creative activities in just a few minutes. Use these eyebolts, along with ropes and pulleys, for a variety of fun games that children enjoy as they develop motor skills. The initial effort required to install these inexpensive eyebolts and prepare ropes, bolt snaps, and pulleys will be rewarded over the following years each time you are able to quickly set up seemingly complicated activities in just a few minutes. Read on to learn how to add pulleys to play Go Fish, add scooters to play Scooter Pull, and add cloth draped over the rope to play a variety of net games.

Go Fish

Muscular strength and endurance

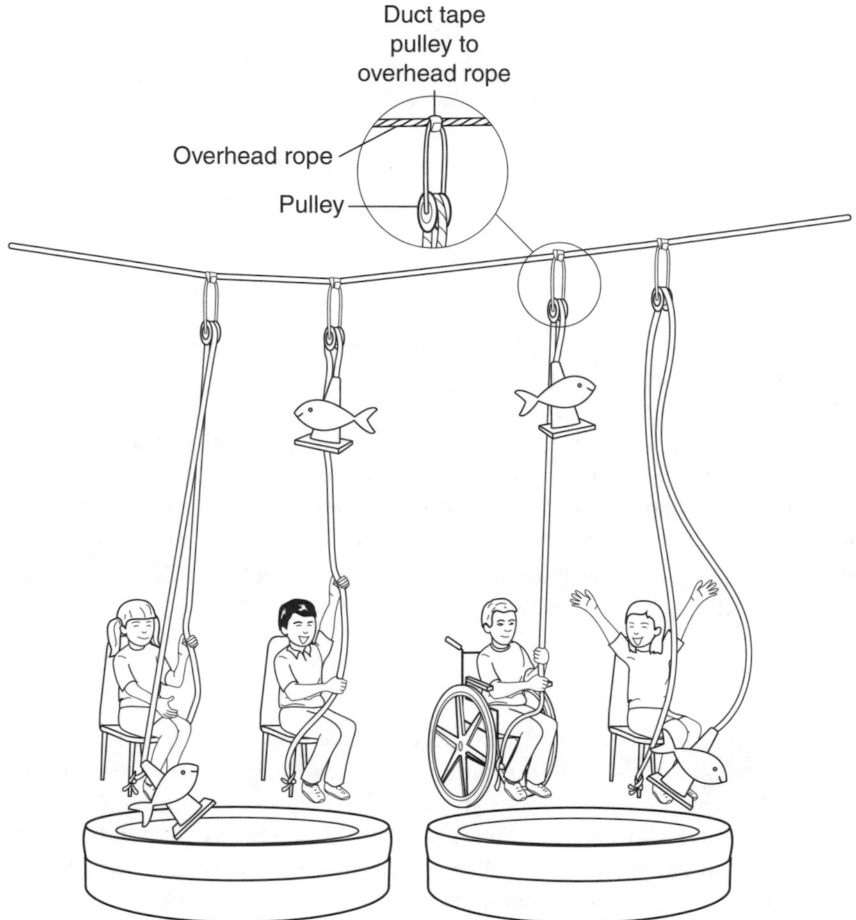

Adapted, by permission, from R. McCall and D. Craft, 2000, *Moving with a purpose: Developing programs for preschoolers of all abilities* (Champaign, IL: Human Kinetics), 72.

Screw an eyebolt into a beam in the ceiling of the room; then attach a small pulley to the bolt. This one-time, permanent installation will enable you to quickly set up for Go Fish for years to come. Pass the clothesline rope through the single pulley. Tie one end of the rope to the leg of a chair in which a child sits to prevent it from slipping out through the pulley. Attach a weighted object to the other end; then go fishing.

Overview

This activity is a variation of Hand-Over-Hand Pull found in the book *Moving With a Purpose* (McCall and Craft 2000). Use a rope, an eyebolt, and a small pulley to "go fishing." The children pull hand over hand on a rope to lift up and reel in the weighted fish they catch. They then let go of the rope to let the fish drop, pretending that they are releasing it and letting the fish swim away. It is a fun way to develop upper body strength.

Goals for Children

- Develop upper body strength and endurance
- Learn to pull with a hand-over-hand motion
- Practice grasping and releasing

Equipment

For only one or two children, make one fishing station from the following materials:

- One three-inch (8 cm) eyebolt, attached to the ceiling
- One two-inch (5 cm) small metal pulley, attached to the ceiling eyebolt
- One length of rope, twice the distance from the ceiling to the floor
- One soft, weighted object, such as a three- to five-pound (1-1/2 to 2-1/2 kg) sport cone, attached to one end of the rope
- One picture of a fish, or an inflatable pool toy in the shape of a fish, attached to the weighted object to reinforce the fishing theme.
- A designated area for the object to fall, such as a plastic wading pool or large box
- One chair
- Fishing music (see suggestions under "Instructions")
- CD player

Equipment Tips

Eyebolts, pulleys, and ropes are easy to find and inexpensive to purchase at hardware stores. Follow the protocol in your program. You may be expected to request permission from your building administrator and assistance from the custodial staff to install the required eyebolts.

Preparation

Thread a length of clothesline that is cut to twice the distance from the overhead pulley to the floor. Tie a knot to make a loop at one end of the rope, and slip it around the chair leg. Tie the other end of the rope securely to a soft, weighted object of three to five pounds. If using a plastic cone, punch a hole near the top of the cone, and thread the rope through and tie it securely. Place a plastic wading pool, large box, or other container under the rope so that the weighted object falls into it when the rope is released. If you wish, put plastic fish in the pool or box to create a stimulating starting position and add to the fishing theme. Place the chair at the desired distance from the object to be hoisted, and place the object to be lifted in the starting position inside the pool or box. Now children can see where the weighted object is to land each time they release the rope. Your fishing station is now complete.

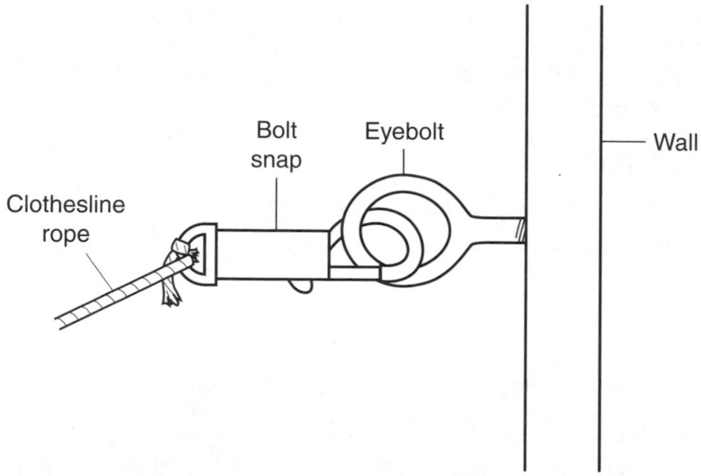

Instructions

1. Ask a child to sit in the chair. Demonstrate how to grasp the rope and pull it using a hand-over-hand motion to hoist the weighted object upward. Pretend that the rope is a fishing pole and that the child is reeling in a big fish.
2. When the object reaches the pulley at the top of the rope, the child releases the rope so that the object falls into the pool or box. Pretend that the fish has just been released back into the water.
3. Create a border around the area to remind children not to enter where the fish drops. Use a bench or mat to create a safe barrier. Instruct children not to cross the border. Provide close adult supervision for this activity.
4. Review these safety rules:
   - Stay away from the weighted object.
   - Wait for a turn in a designated area, or go to an alternative activity.
   - Do not step into the area where the weighted object is falling.
   - To avoid rope burns, quickly open hands to release the rope.
5. Provide fishing hats (if available) for children to wear, and play upbeat music with a fishing or ocean theme such as the song "Blanket for a Sail" by Harry Nilsson on the CD *Legendary Harry Nilsson* from DJ Specialist and available through www.amazon.com. These props and songs further increase children's enthusiasm and willingness to hoist long after their muscles begin to fatigue.
6. Turn on the music and let the fishing begin!

Adaptations

Children of all abilities can participate in this activity. Place a child unable to sit independently in a mobile prone stander, tumble form chair, Rifton chair, or wheelchair. Assist children with limited grip strength by tying knots an equal distance apart along the rope. The knots make it less likely that children's hands will slide back when they grasp.

Variations

- Increase the weight attached to the rope.
- Use a timer with a buzzer to add motivation. Challenge children to hoist the fish up before the time runs out and the buzzer goes off. Be sure that the children always beat the timer.
- Change the name of the game to Hoist the Crane. Have the children pretend that the rope, eyebolt, and small pulley make a working crane instead of a fishing pole. Children use the crane to hoist a weight, then let it fall. Provide hard hats, either real or paper imitations, for children to wear as they imagine they are controlling the cranes at a construction site. Encouraging the children to imagine themselves as construction workers only increases their motivation to continue hoisting the weighted object and increases their upper body strength.
- Change the name of the game to Animal Climbing Rope. Attach a stuffed animal, instead of a fish, to the end of the rope. Have the children pretend that the animal is "climbing" the rope as they hoist it into the air. Then have them imagine that the animal is jumping back down as they release the rope. Children enjoy these and other themes.

Changing the Space

- In a small space, conduct the activity as described earlier.
- In a large space, add more fishing stations by suspending a rope overhead horizontally between two eyebolts fastened seven feet up on opposing or adjacent walls across the open space up to 25 feet (8 m) wide. Attach pulleys and ropes to the horizontal rope to create four or five stations at which children can fish. Multiple pulleys on one horizontal rope must be held in place by putting duct tape on both sides of each pulley so that they will not shift their position along the rope. This keeps the stations a safe distance apart.
- Outdoors, suspend the overhead rope between two trees or clothesline poles; then attach pulleys, ropes, and weighted objects. Alternatively, remove the swings from a standard swing set and throw a rope over the horizontal beam at the top of the swing set. You now have a quick, simpler version of the fishing station that requires neither a pulley nor an eyebolt. Fill the plastic wading pool with water and perform the fishing activity outside on warm days. Children love the big splash that happens when the weighted object drops back into the pool.

Scooter Pull

Muscular strength and endurance

A long rope, three eyebolts, and scooters will have children pulling themselves on their bellies through a scooter course. Add tunnels under which they pass, and you have a novel, motivating way to build upper body strength.

Overview

Here is a second use of ropes and eyebolts. Mount three eyebolts on opposing walls three inches above the floor; then string a clothesline rope through the eyebolts. This taut rope serves as a scooter pull course. Once the eyebolts are installed and the ropes cut, finish each rope end with a bolt snap to secure it to an eyebolt. This is a very easy activity to set up each day. Just unwrap the ropes, clip them on the eyebolts, and have children pull themselves along the rope course on scooters for a fun upper body–strengthening activity. Scooter Pull is one variation of Scooter Play found in *Moving With a Purpose* (McCall and Craft 2000, 114).

Goals for Children

- Develop upper body strength
- Learn to pull using a hand-over-hand motion

Equipment

- One scooter per child
- Minimum of three large eyebolts
- Two bolt snaps, small enough to pass through the large eyebolts
- Clothesline rope (the length required depends on the space available); use cotton rope because, unlike nylon rope, it does not stretch very much
- Mats, boxes, tables, or anything to create safe tunnels under which children can scoot
- CD of lively music
- CD player

Equipment Tips

Scooters can be purchased at larger toy stores or through physical activity catalogs such as FlagHouse (www.flaghouse.com) or Sportime (www.sportime.com). Clothesline rope and eyebolts are available at hardware stores. Consider asking a parent group or another support organization for funds to purchase these supplies.

Be sure that the bolt snaps are large enough to snap onto the eyebolts, but small enough to fit through the eyebolts if threading the rope through several eyebolts is the goal.

Preparation

Plan a scooter rope course that stretches at least 25 feet (8 m) across the activity room to create a triangle, square, zigzag, or other multisided shape. Plan at least three sides to your shape, using at least three eyebolts. Avoid simply creating one straight line that uses only two eyebolts and forces children to scoot only down and back while trying to negotiate around oncoming children; this can create bottlenecks and frustration. At each angle of the shape, screw a large eyebolt into the wall about three inches above the floor. This one-time installation will save hours of preparation in the future!

Next, check that the bolt snaps are small enough to pass through the large eyebolts. Tie one end of the rope to a bolt snap; then attach the bolt snap to the first eyebolt. Create your scooter course by threading the rope through as many eyebolts as you have attached to the walls, finishing back at the first eyebolt. Measure, cut, and attach the second bolt snap to the cut end of the rope; then clip it onto the eyebolt that terminates the course. Check that the rope is stretched taut when both ends are clipped to the eyebolts.

Consider creating tunnels from boxes, tables draped with cloth, or mats supported by blocks. Use anything that is at hand and safe to create tunnels for children to pass under as they pull themselves through the scooter course.

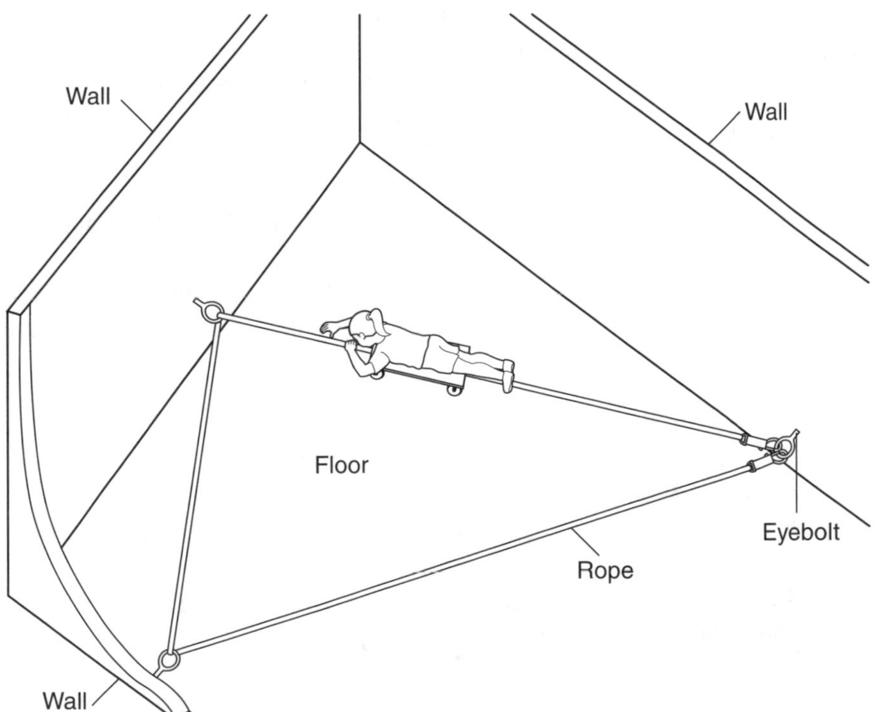

Illustration shows proper setup but is not drawn in proportion; each rope must be at least 25 feet long.

Instructions

1. Demonstrate how the children are to lie on their bellies on scooters, grasp the rope in their hands, and pull themselves along the course using a hand-over-hand motion.
2. Review scooter safety. Remind children to sit or lie, but not stand, on the scooters. Also caution them to keep their hands from under the scooters so that they do not run over their fingers. Children who are moving quickly may pick up and carry their scooters around children who are moving more slowly, but there should be no pushing. When finished with the scooter course, instruct children to return their scooters to the scooter garage, which you have clearly marked with a cartoon character.
3. Turn on the music and let the children begin pulling themselves through the scooter course.

Adaptations

For children able to do the hand-over-hand pulling motion but unable to use a standard scooter, substitute a long scooter, padded scooter, Jettmobile, or tumble form chair on a wheeled platform. Place children unable to propel themselves on adapted scooters that allow them the most comfort and facilitate their movement. Facilitate the children's hand-over-hand pulling motion using the cues "grasp-pull-release." Alternatively, give them a hula hoop to grasp while you hold the opposite side of the hoop and pull them through the course as they sit on a scooter, tumble form chair on wheels, or whatever equipment you devise to meet their needs.

Variations

- Add ramps for the children to negotiate.
- Have the children close their eyes and try to place their hands on the rope and pull.
- Add a time challenge to see how fast the children can complete the scooter course. This should not be a race against each other, but rather a group race against the clock.

Changing the Space

- In a small space, decrease the number of eyebolts used to create a smaller course. Be sure to have at least three angles in the course.
- In a larger space, increase the challenge of the course and the directions created.
- This activity will work outdoors if blacktop space is available with trees or poles to which you can attach the rope.

Nets, Targets, and Balls

Object control

Here is a fun way to motivate young children to practice throwing. Just two eyebolts mounted three feet up on opposite walls can hold a net hung off a stretched rope for a variety of ball games. Place colorful smiley faces or plastic bottles with bells as targets on the other side of the net that is approximately waist-high on the children. Provide a container full of balls so that children can throw for several minutes without stopping.

Overview

Screw two eyebolts in the wall at three feet above the floor. Attach a taut rope between them, and drape a bedsheet over the rope. Now you have a net to use in a variety of ball games. Children stand on one side of the net and throw over the net at targets. Vary the size of, and distance to, the targets to fit the skill level of the children. The net reminds children where to stand when throwing and reduces the danger of their getting hit by running in front of others who are throwing.

Goals for Children

- Develop eye–hand coordination

Equipment

- Two eyebolts
- Two bolt snaps, small enough to pass through the large eyebolts
- One long cotton rope (rather than nylon rope to avoid stretching the rope) that extends from one wall or support across the open space to the opposite wall or support, with the exact length dependent on the size of the open space
- Sheet, tablecloth, parachute, or other lightweight fabric to drape over the rope
- Many soft balls of various sizes, such as old tennis balls, paper balls (wad paper into a ball and then wrap in masking tape to help it retain its shape), foam balls, Koosh balls, beach balls, or even paper plates. Allow at least 25 balls per child so that everyone can throw several times without having to wait for a ball.
- Plastic bottles, paper smiley faces, bins, boxes, or other targets
- Small jingle bells
- CD of lively music
- CD player

Equipment Tips

- You may want to use only one type of ball for a given activity. Use either heavier tennis balls or very light paper balls in the activity, but not both at the same time. It requires little time and money to wad paper to make 100 paper balls that are lightweight and can be carried in a large garbage bag.
- Seek donations of old balls from parents or community members.
- Use any lightweight fabric from your classroom or home to drape over the rope to create a net.
- Eyebolts, ropes, and bolt snaps are available from hardware stores.
- When the activity is finished and you have removed the ropes, cover the eyebolts to prevent children from running into them. Old fluorescent-colored tennis balls with slits cut in them big enough to slide over the eyebolts make excellent covers. Another approach is to mount a permanent protector surrounding the eyebolt. Cut the center out of a thick piece of foam, and place the foam over the eyebolt, gluing it to the wall. Be sure that the foam is thick and firm enough so that a person who might fall would strike only the foam surrounding the eyebolt and not the eyebolt itself.
- Novelty beanbags can be purchased from Constructive Playthings (www.cptoys.com).

Preparation

When making a net, determine the open space in the center of the activity area across which you wish to suspend a rope and create a net. Choose a spot for your net. On opposite walls, screw one eyebolt into each wall at the point three feet (1 m) above the floor. Tie a bolt snap to one end of the clothesline rope. Then stretch the rope across the open space to the opposite eyebolt. Pull the rope across the open space; then measure, cut, and tie the other end of the rope to the other bolt snap. When the bolt snap is attached to the second eyebolt, the rope needs to be stretched taut. Now drape lightweight fabric over the rope to form a net about three feet (1 m)

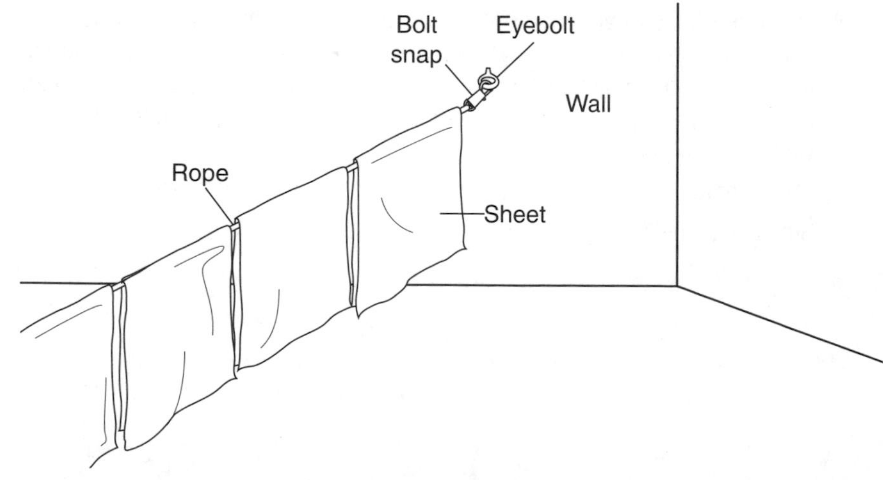

high across the open space. Remember to provide a large bin full of balls to throw. Children become very motivated when they see a large bin full of balls that will take the entire class time to empty.

To make targets, use any of the following ideas:

- Make targets from empty two-liter plastic soda bottles. Suspend targets, from the ceiling or from a rope stretched horizontally and overhead, by tying ropes around the necks of the bottles. Children can throw and hit the targets again and again without waiting for you to reset these targets. This allows continuous fun for the children and frees you to give children feedback on throwing skills. Attach jingle bells to the bottles to increase motivation. Children love to hear the bells ring when they have hit the target.
- Look in a fabric store for fabric depicting oversized prints of favorite characters such as Bob the Builder or Scooby Doo. Purchase one square yard of this fabric. Duct tape or sew one side of the fabric to a wooden dowel to create a banner. Suspend the banner as a target for children to hit with balls.
- Make a paper target by cutting out a large paper smiley face. Secure it to the wall, a large mat, or a suspended sheet.
- Make a plywood target in the shape of a favorite character. Cut out holes in the wooden character through which the children can throw objects. If you don't own the needed tools, ask a relative, neighbor, or technology teacher at school to cut the holes.
- Create yet another target from a Little Tykes climber or similar equipment by removing the slide, covering the openings around the side with paper, and using it as a huge container into which children throw objects. To create a construction theme with the target, put pictures of Bob the Builder on the paper that surrounds the climber. As children throw balls into the climber, they can pretend they are loading the bed of a dump truck. Or, use a winter theme, and have the children pretend to throw snow into a snow removal truck.
- Use a window shade to make a novel target. Draw or paint a colorful picture on the window shade to match the theme of the activity you are doing. Mount the shade on brackets in a location where it can be left there permanently to save time during future activities. Pull the shade down for the activity; then raise it when you finish. Make several shades with different pictures. One example is to throw dinosaur beanbags at a shade with a picture of a dinosaur on it. Switch shades quickly and easily as you change activity themes. You can leave the shade down as children hit it with beanbags. Or, you can give a quick tug on the shade when it is hit so that it retracts. Children love to be startled as the shade snaps up after they hit it.

Primary school children may be ready to throw at relatively small targets such as plastic bottles. As an alternative to throwing at bottles, try having them throw balls into large rubber storage tubs or plastic wading pools instead of traditional targets.

Getting the balls into these tubs or pools requires less accuracy than throwing at targets. Tubs and pools also have the benefit of making cleanup easier. Simply pour the balls out of the tub or pool into the storage container, or even store the balls in the tub.

Instructions

1. With everyone on one side of the net, present the children with boxes full of old tennis balls, paper balls, foam balls, or Koosh balls. Make sure there are plenty of balls for the children to use so that no one must wait for a ball. Because repetition is the key to skill development, children need many, many opportunities to throw in this activity.
2. Set up targets on the other side of the net. Vary the distances to the targets from 2 feet to 10 feet (1 to 3 m). Children will tend to position themselves in front of the net opposite a target that presents them with a reasonable challenge. Always provide targets to keep children focused on throwing at something. Otherwise children may become bored and begin to throw balls at each other or randomly around the room. If you keep the children's attention focused on the target, then that is where the balls will go.
3. Turn on some lively music and let the children begin throwing.

Adaptations

Children of all abilities can participate in this activity. A child unable to stand independently can be placed in a mobile prone stander, gait trainer, tumble form chair, or wheelchair, depending on the circumstance (see figure 1.1 on page 10).

Children at the rudimentary phase of development will need practice grasping and releasing objects. They are not yet ready to throw for distance. Position these children close to the net. Place a motivating target directly below them on the other side of the net. Challenge them to drop the ball over the net onto the target.

Variations

- Vary the targets at which children throw. Many different targets were explained previously.
- Play this fun volleyball lead-up activity. Position the children on both sides of the net, facing each other. For young children who are not ready for a structured game of volleyball, have plenty of balls available and let the children simply volley, bat, or catch and then throw the balls back and forth over the net. Avoid using tennis balls or other firm objects because the children are throwing the balls to each other. Choose from a variety of lightweight balls including beach balls, paper balls, foam balls, or the more expensive AirLite, or small- to medium-size Omnikin balls. AirLite balls may be purchased from FlagHouse (www.flaghouse.com), and Omnikin balls from Omnikin, Inc. (www.omnikin.com) in Canada.

- In another variation, have children on both sides of the net throw soft objects across the net to each other. This activity can be played as the game Garbage Cleanup described in *Moving With a Purpose* (McCall and Craft 2000, 68-69). The object is to clean out your side of the "backyard" by throwing all of the objects over the net before children on the other side of the net can throw them back into your yard.
- Increase the challenge in any of these activities by increasing the distance the children throw the ball and decreasing the size of the target.
- Hold a snowball fight using very light foam balls to throw over the net. The three-inch lightweight foam spacers that are used to pack fruit are ideal for this activity. As an added bonus these spacers are white and actually look a bit like snowballs. This activity can be a fun way to practice throwing during the winter months, but also in warm weather and in warm climates just for the novelty.

Changing the Space

- In a smaller space, create a shorter net and limit the number of children participating at one time. Use very lightweight balls such as beach balls, foam balls, or paper balls if playing the activity in a small classroom.
- In a larger space, increase the net size, the number of children participating, and the number of balls used.
- This is a great activity for outdoors. Suspend the rope between trees or poles. Attach the rope to the tree or pole using a bungee cord.

chapter 6

Use Your Noodles

Nathan had always used plastic bats for children to practice batting and as bars for children to practice jumping over. Yet, he found that occasionally a child would cry when accidentally hit with a bat swung by a classmate. Nathan also was not happy with the rigidity of plastic bats when children landed directly on them after an unsuccessful jump over the hurdle. He wanted something softer and flexible to serve as a bat and hurdle bar. While browsing through the local dollar store, he noticed foam pool noodles for sale. He instantly realized that pool noodles could be cut in varying lengths to make perfect soft striking implements. He was delighted to realize that they would also do double duty as a hurdle for children to jump over and as a bar for children to grasp while jumping in place.

AFFORDABLE, COLORFUL FOAM NOODLES can be modified to create stimulating activities to help three- to seven-year-olds develop the gross motor skills of striking and jumping. Here are three safe, kid-tested activities that are easy to prepare.

Swing Your Noodle Bat

Object control

This easy-to-assemble activity allows children to practice batting a cloth-covered balloon or other soft object again and again, without the need to pause to chase or reposition the object being struck. The ball or other suspended object simply swings back into place in front of the child, ready to be struck again.

Overview

Young children need the chance to learn to swing a bat. Foam noodles are a soft alternative to plastic bats for practicing this skill.

Goals for Children

- Develop striking skills
- Develop eye–hand coordination

Equipment

- Pool noodles
- Soft balls or cloth-covered balloons for batting
- Floor spots
- CD of lively music
- CD player

Equipment Tips

- Affordable, colorful foam noodles are typically sold in dollar stores, craft supply stores, and stores that carry pool toys. They are also sold in the toy section of large discount stores. Noodles are typically sold in four- to six-foot lengths (1 to 2 m) for a dollar each. Because they are seasonal items, the best time to stock up on them is at the beginning of summer.
- Floor spots can be purchased from sport supply catalogs. A cheaper alternative is plastic place mats. Select ones with nonskid backing. If foot traffic will be heavy, you may want to keep them in position using duct tape.

Preparation

Noodles come in various lengths, so they need to be cut to accommodate the height of the children using them. Shorter children may be more successful batting with two-foot lengths, and taller children, with three-foot (1 m) lengths. Noodles that are four, five, and six feet long can be cut in half to make two- to three-foot lengths (1 m). For a child with particularly small hands, create a smaller grip by carving away foam pieces at one end of the noodle until it fits comfortably in the child's grasp.

Refer to page 61 in chapter 5 for an explanation of how to suspend a rope overhead across the room.

To make a batting target, place a soft foam ball in a bag or cloth covering, or encase a balloon in a commercially made cloth covering called a Balzac. To enable several children to bat simultaneously, suspend five or six targets, one for each child at the children's chest height, along a horizontally suspended rope. Use an eyebolt in the ceiling or yarn attached to a rope strung overhead parallel to the floor. Space the targets along the rope so that the children will naturally stand away from each other while striking.

Mark a spot on the floor to indicate where each child stands while batting. Most preschool children need to stand close to the side of each suspended target. Primary school children may be able to stand a short distance away so that they can get a mature swing. Making a floor spot can be as simple as taping an X on the floor. For more interest, use colorful, nonskid place mats as floor spots.

Young children might be unsuccessful in their first attempts at striking. Before giving corrective feedback, give children an opportunity to swing a few times to feel success even with less-than-perfect form. Striking a suspended ball is much easier than batting a pitched ball. Keeping two hands on the bat may be all that beginning batters are ready to handle. As their skill progresses throughout the year, instruct them in hand placement, noting whether they are showing right- or left-hand dominance. Still later, prompt children to place the bat above their shoulder to begin, and to swing in a big circle around their tummy. Some children may eventually be ready to learn specific foot placement and weight shift.

Instructions

1. Instruct children to stay on their own floor spots. This serves as a visual prompt to keep them in their own spaces, safely away from other children who are also swinging noodle bats.
2. Demonstrate correct striking form; then let the children begin batting.
3. Turn on lively music to stimulate movement.
4. As they are swinging, facilitate the correct striking form.

Adaptations

Place children who may not be able to stand independently in mobile prone standers or gait trainers (see figure 1.1 on page 10). The adapted equipment allows the children to be supported in upright positions, with their hands free for batting. Children seated in wheelchairs can be positioned next to the suspended object and join in for batting practice. Remember to check that the wheelchair brake is on before a child starts batting.

Variations

- Use the noodle to bat a foam ball off a large cone or tee ball stand.
- Challenge the children to bat a beach ball or small Omnikin ball along the floor.
- For children with very advanced striking skills, gently pitch a soft foam ball to them for batting practice.

Changing the Space

- In a small space, suspend only one target ball or balloon for batting practice.
- In a large space, have several children bat at the same time. Suspend the objects to be batted at least three feet apart, mark the floor spots to keep the children apart, and let the swinging begin. If contact with another child does occur, it will be with a soft noodle, not a plastic bat.
- This activity will be just as easy to set up outdoors. Suspend the balls or balloons from the horizontal pole of a swing set or a sturdy tree branch.

Jumping the Hurdles

Locomotor skills • Object, color, and shape recognition

This is a safe, enjoyable way for children to develop the skill of jumping, whether you are using a big or small space.

Overview

Use your noodles to create hurdles for a lesson in jumping. Tape them on the floor or on low supports such as foam shape holders. Vary the height of the hurdles based on the children's jumping skills. Use only soft objects for support so that there is no worry of injury if the children hit the hurdles while learning to jump (see the equipment list for ideas). Select noodles of varying colors, diameters, and shapes (straight, creased, or coiled), and you've added a lesson in color, size, and shape recognition.

Goals for Children

- Develop the skill of jumping over objects

Equipment

- Foam noodles, cut into two- to three-foot (1 m) lengths
- Duct tape

- Pairs of cones, foam shape holders, or other soft objects on which to place each noodle, raising the noodles several inches off the floor
- CD of lively music
- CD player

Equipment Tips

Refer to the description of Swing Your Noodle Bat for equipment tips (page 72).

Preparation

Use the noodles to create hurdles over which the children practice jumping. For a low jump, lay the noodle directly on the carpet or matted floor, using duct tape to keep it in place. For a raised jump, attach each end of the noodle to a cone or other soft, raised object, securing it in place with duct tape.

Space six to eight hurdles in a large circle or square, allowing at least two feet between hurdles. Form a continuous path of hurdles for the children to follow around and around.

Instructions

1. Demonstrate the skill of jumping. For safety, demonstrate and teach all children to jump in the same direction.
2. Turn on the lively music and let the children start jumping.
3. Children will approach the jumps at varying speeds and ability levels. It is fine if one child laps the course repeatedly in the same time span that other children require to complete one journey through the course. Hold the children's attention by allowing them the freedom to negotiate the course at their own pace.

Adaptations

Prop some of the hurdles high enough so that nonambulatory children, and all of their friends, can crawl underneath them.

Variations

- Encourage children at the initial stage of jumping to simply step over the hurdles. Offer support to children who are capable of stepping over the hurdles but need encouragement before doing so independently. As children become more skilled, encourage them to increase the bend in their knees and the swing in their arms to jump rather than step over the hurdles.
- Offer a variety of heights within the same jumping course to challenge both novice and skilled jumpers. Allow the children to decide which heights they feel ready to jump. Gently encourage skilled children to attempt higher hurdles.
- Add something silly to motivate the children even more. Place a motion-sensitive frog or dog ornament on the landing side of each hurdle. The frog will croak or the dog will bark as each child lands the jump over the hurdle. Children love this!
- Create a jumping path that takes on a square or curving road pattern. Let the children negotiate the path as they jump. With a square path, the children can change direction before they come to the next hurdle. With a more challenging curved path, children need to change direction as they jump each hurdle.
- Create a high jump using a six-foot (2 m) pool noodle. Place padding underneath to cushion any falls. Assist any children who might have difficulty lifting their legs over the noodle high jump bar, such as some children with cerebral palsy.

Changing the Space

- In a small space, limit the number of hurdles used.
- In a large space, increase the number of hurdles used.
- Outdoors, set up a jumping course on the grass.

Suspended Noodle Jump

Locomotor skills • Cardiovascular endurance

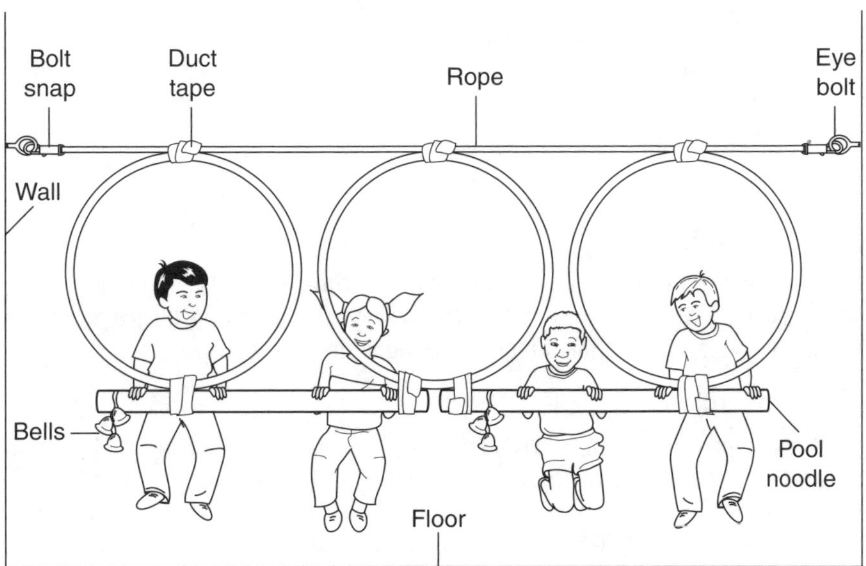

Children will jump all day, using this very inexpensive arrangement of rope, pool noodles, hula hoops, and jingle bells. The apparatus is flexible and safe, and it gives as children jump at differing times and heights.

Overview

Simply jumping in place can be boring and tiring for children. To add variety and interest, suspend a noodle at waist height parallel to the floor. This way children can grasp it as they jump. Attach bells that jingle as the noodle moves, and play lively music. Now you have children eager to jump up and down continuously, delighting in making the bells ring.

Goals for Children

- Develop jumping skills
- Increase cardiovascular fitness
- Practice sharing space

Equipment

- Pool noodles (one noodle for every two children)
- Rope
- Bells
- Hula hoops
- Duct tape
- CD of lively music with a clear beat
- CD player

Equipment Tips

You can purchase rope in discount department stores or dollar stores, and jingle bells are in the craft sections of discount stores. Purchasing single bells may be less expensive; you can string them together using yarn.

Preparation

Noodles are made into horizontally suspended bars, waist high on the children, with noisemakers attached. The arrangement, shown at the beginning of this activity, can accommodate four or five children at once. Begin by suspending a taut rope overhead. Refer to page 61 in chapter 5 for instructions for suspending the long rope overhead. Lower the long overhead rope down to the floor and attach shorter ropes at two- or three-foot (1 m) intervals. Next, use duct tape to attach the hula hoops to the rope. Then, tape each noodle to the bottom of the hula hoops. Tie bells or other noisemakers to the noodles. Hoist the long rope overhead across the room, adjusting the height so that the attached noodles are suspended at waist level for children to grab. The bells will ring, the hoops will jiggle, and the children will jump for minutes at a time without stopping.

Instructions

1. Demonstrate how to grab the noodle suspended at waist level in front of each child. Then show how to jump up and down in place. The motivation of the bells ringing and the security of holding the noodle for balance result in children's enjoyment of the practice of this skill.
2. Turn on lively music with a clear beat. Encourage children as they jump and jingle.

Adaptation

A child unable to stand independently can be placed in a gait trainer or mobile prone stander for support. This frees the child to grasp and shake the noodle by moving the hands back and forth. This is a very motivating activity for working on range of motion and developing upper body strength.

Variation

The arrangement shown in figure 6.1 is for suspending just one noodle to be used by one child at a time. This activity requires an overhead support such as a beam, strong tree limb, crossbar on a swing set (with swings removed), or two eyebolts firmly secured in the ceiling. Suspend two ropes from the overhead support so that they extend to about waist height on a child. Tie the dangling ends of the rope to either end of the pool noodle so that the noodle is suspended at a child's waist height. Attach noisemakers such as jingle bells to the rope.

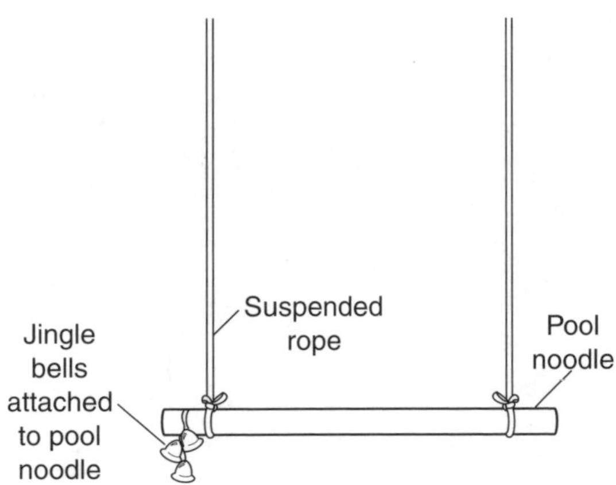

Figure 6.1 One noodle suspended from an overhead support for one child to use.

Changing the Space

- In a small space, suspend one noodle as an individual jumping station.
- In a large space, suspend several noodles and hula hoops as described earlier. You may also use uncut six-foot (2 m) noodles to accommodate several children at once.
- Outdoors, suspend the noodles from the horizontal pole of a swing set or a safe, sturdy tree branch.

chapter 7

Roll a Veggie, Toss a Fruit

Mrs. Schultz was observing a group of young children throwing. She noticed that while they were trying to enjoy themselves, the activity seemed to have become as old and routine as the beanbags they were throwing. She approached Joey to ask why he was not as enthusiastic as he was normally. He replied that he loved to throw, but was bored with always throwing beanbags. Mrs. Schultz didn't want to lose the spark these children had for learning, so she knew she needed to find a more motivating way to have them practice the skill of throwing.

KEEP THE BALLS AND BEANBAGS in the closet. For exciting motivation, invite children to throw real potatoes (see the note in the following paragraph about safety issues), play catch with a partner using plastic fruit, or roll a seedless watermelon along the floor. These are just three of the food play ideas that will have small children laughing themselves silly as they practice throwing, catching, and rolling.

Young children are typically at the initial stage of throwing and have not yet learned how to throw hard. If you have a child who can throw an object with enough force to hurt or cause the fruit or vegetable to go splat, use only soft beanbag fruit and vegetables instead of real ones. As a precaution, remind children not to eat the foods used in the games.

You can create your own food theme by designating the objects to be handled and the type of target. Arrange the area so that children are throwing toward a target from behind a barrier, rolling down an incline, or standing on a floor spot while tossing and catching with partners. The food combination possibilities are endless. Your equipment list is limited only by your culinary imagination. Just keep it safe and always have boundaries.

Fruit Salad

Object control

Who wants to always throw old beanbags at targets? Enliven your lesson by having the children throw fruit, real or plastic, into a container. Children delight in pretending they are making a fruit salad.

Overview

A popular activity with children is making fruit salad by throwing stuffed or plastic fruit into a large bowl.

Goals for Children

- Develop eye–hand coordination
- Practice object identification

Equipment

- Real tiny pumpkins, stuffed fabric fruit, or plastic fruit
- A large container such as a large box, bin, plastic swimming pool, or inverted tumble top used as a bin
- Bins, tubs, or other objects to create a barrier (see notes under "Preparation")

- CD of upbeat music
- CD player

Equipment Tips

Stuffed fabric and plastic fruit and vegetables can be found at most discount stores or through the Constructive Playthings catalog (www.cptoys.com) at very reasonable prices. Once purchased, plastic fruit and vegetables will last for years and can be used in a wide variety of activities. Stuffed fabric food typically comes in a character form, with a face and name. Make plastic food more stimulating by using a marker to create a face such as a smiling corn cob or a winking carrot.

Preparation

When using real food, purchase the food as close to the activity day as possible. Potatoes, pumpkins, and other firm foods will usually last through one week of activity. A hard-boiled egg will last until the shell breaks, so have a large supply and play on soft surfaces such as grass or mats.

Children will want to run forward to see the results of their throwing efforts. Keep them safely back from the target by placing a barrier between them and the target. A barrier reduces the chance that someone will get hit with a thrown object. Use large plastic tubs, folded mats, a line of cones, a low-strung rope covered with a sheet, or several bins or boxes that contain the play food to create a barrier behind which the children throw.

Instructions

1. The activity setup will depend on the skill you want the children to practice: either throw and catch, or roll. Be sure to create boundaries. Fabric or plastic fruit placed in bins or boxes in a semicircle in front of the children can create a natural boundary. Folded mats also make excellent boundaries that serve as tables on which to place the objects to be thrown.
2. Explain the activity and teach the children that the boundary means "Stop! Do not cross while others are throwing!" Also explain that each child handles only one food item at a time.
3. Play upbeat music in the background. Use the music as a signal to start and stop the activity.
4. As the children play, facilitate any skill refinement children need and casually repeat expectations to reinforce their learning. Simply saying, "Put your hand by your ear" is an effective cue for young children. Cues such as "stretch" or "reach" also work. Older children might understand the cue, "Stretch your arm as you throw."
5. Motivate the children by repeatedly referring to the food theme and what the children are creating: "What a great-looking salad! Keep adding more fruit!"
6. When children run low on fruit to throw, simply dump the bowl filled with fruit in front of them to keep the activity going.

Adaptations

This activity requires that children's hands be free for throwing. Prop children who are unable to stand so they can sit and play this activity. Alternatively, children unable to walk or stand independently may use adapted equipment such as a gait trainer or mobile prone stander so their hands are not required for support.

Variations

- Potato Salad: Practice the overhand throw by making a potato salad using real potatoes. Buy a bag of potatoes that are thoroughly washed and dried but not peeled. As a bowl, use a large plastic container with sides high enough to contain the thrown potatoes. Establish clear boundaries. Make sure the children understand the instructions and know where to throw. When throwing toward a target, place it close to or against a wall. This decreases the number of thrown objects that go astray. Remember, if you have a child who can throw an object with enough force to hurt or cause the fruit or vegetable to go splat, use only soft beanbag fruit and vegetables instead of real ones in this activity.
- Orange Juice: Instead of having the children throw at a target, have them toss to each other. Make it novel by giving them oranges or other firm, but not hard, real fruit or stuffed or plastic food. Use spot markers to designate where each child is to stand while tossing. The distance between the spot marker and the catcher can easily be adjusted to match each child's throwing skill. Consider using place mats, carpet squares, or laminated pictures as spot markers. Have the spot markers match the food items to emphasize the theme for the activity.

Changing the Space

- In a small space, limit the throwing area and use stuffed or plastic food. Typically 8 to 10 children can participate at the same time in a small, controlled space.
- In a large space, expand the number of items to throw. Increase the size of the target and the area in which the children can move.
- If outdoors, it may be safest to play these activities on grass, setting up the activity in the same manner as indoors.

Pumpkin Bowling

Muscular strength and endurance • Object control

Children love wacky activities that use familiar objects in novel ways. Bowling with pumpkins instead of balls is just such an activity.

Overview

One at a time, children roll a real pumpkin down a small slide and knock over a plastic pumpkin. They then slide down and retrieve the real pumpkin. It is a great way to

practice climbing and rolling. Plus, as the children carry the pumpkin back to the starting place and hand it to an adult, they will be exercising their muscles!

Goals for Children

- Develop object control
- Develop muscular strength
- Develop climbing skills

Equipment

- A real six- to eight-inch pumpkin
- A large plastic pumpkin, about three feet tall
- A small incline or slide
- Two two-by-four (50 mm × 100 mm, sanded framing timber; or flatter and wider) boards or other barriers placed on either side to form a runway (optional)

Equipment Tips

Many playground toys for young children include a small plastic slide. This slide can be used as an incline for rolling the pumpkin. Place a long two-by-four (50 mm × 100 mm, sanded framing timber; or flatter and wider) board or other barrier on each side of the runway to create a bowling alley with bumpers.

Preparation

Create a slide for the real pumpkin to roll down to hit the plastic pumpkin positioned five feet (2 m) in front of the slide.

Instructions

1. Place a real pumpkin in position at the top of a small slide and a plastic pumpkin about five feet (2 m) from the bottom of the slide.
2. The child climbs the ladder and pushes the pumpkin down the slide to try to knock over the plastic pumpkin at the bottom.
3. The child then follows the pumpkin down the slide, retrieves the real pumpkin, and carries it back to the slide for an adult to put it at the starting place for the next child's turn. Meanwhile, an adult resets the plastic pumpkin. Alternatively, children who are capable can reset their own pumpkins.

Adaptations

Help children who are unable to climb independently by facilitating or physically assisting them with climbing motion. With those who may use a wheelchair, position an incline in front of the wheelchair, so they can push the pumpkin off the incline instead of the slide.

Variations

- Substitute a seedless watermelon for a pumpkin to create a fun summer activity.
- Try the game Roll the Pumpkin described in *Moving With a Purpose* (McCall and Craft 2000, 106-107).

Changing the Space

- In a small classroom space without a child's slide, substitute a wooden board placed on an incline from a table to the floor. The children lift the pumpkin up onto the table, and then push it down the incline to knock over the plastic pumpkin at the bottom.
- In a large space, have Pumpkin Bowling as one of two or three stations available for children to choose.
- The same activity can be played outdoors using a slide on the playground or an incline on a picnic table.

Pumpkins Galore

Muscular strength and endurance • Object control
Motor planning • Locomotor skills
Object, color, and shape recognition

A typical classroom curriculum for young children includes the celebration of autumn with pumpkins, whether through a field trip to a pumpkin patch or arrangements for pumpkins to be delivered to the school or center. Coordinate the movement

curriculum with these classroom activities. Add a special week to your program in which movement activities involve the use of real pumpkins!

Overview

Here are some variations of activities presented elsewhere, all changed to use pumpkins as the theme. Use real pumpkins for extra fun. Set up two or more stations from among the many stations described here.

- Station 1: Pumpkin Bowling, a fun way to practice climbing and rolling
- Station 2: Roll the Pumpkin, with children rolling pumpkins to each other
- Station 3: Pumpkin Gutter Ball, which involves rolling miniature pumpkins down a gutter (see chapter 8 for more on gutter games)
- Station 4: Move and Seek, with miniature pumpkins hidden under cones
- Station 5: Pumpkin Obstacle Course, in which children negotiate around pumpkins and other objects

Conduct Pumpkins Galore on an autumn day when you've invited parents to visit your movement program, as described in chapter 13 on page 194.

Goals for Children

- Develop object control including grasp and release, rolling, and throwing
- Develop muscular strength
- Develop climbing skills

- Develop visual tracking and anticipatory timing
- Develop the ability to match and recall information
- Develop the ability to jump over and negotiate around obstacles

Equipment

- CD of lively music
- CD player
- Station 1—Pumpkin Bowling: A real six- to eight-inch (16 to 20 cm) pumpkin, a large plastic pumpkin, a small incline or slide, and barriers placed on either side of the runway
- Station 2—Roll the Pumpkin: One large pumpkin
- Station 3—Pumpkin Gutter Ball: Vinyl house gutters and elbow joints, stands to support gutters, many miniature pumpkins or small orange balls, and two collection boxes
- Station 4—Move and Seek: One dozen small gym cones or 22-ounce opaque drink cups, several miniature pumpkins that fit under the cones or cups
- Station 5—Pumpkin Obstacle Course: Foam noodles cut into two- to three-foot (1 m) lengths, duct tape, pairs of cones to raise the noodles several inches off the floor, large real or plastic pumpkins

Equipment Tips

Refer to the "Instructions" section that follows for equipment tips.

Preparation

Create stations that relate to the pumpkin theme. Plan only one station that will require close adult supervision and others that can be conducted safely with general supervision.

Instructions

Briefly explain the stations, keeping these comments to a maximum of three minutes to prevent restlessness among young children. Invite children to go to whichever station they wish and change stations whenever they wish. Giving children the freedom to choose what they want to do and when they want to change will eliminate a host of behavior difficulties. Play lively music to signal that children may begin playing at the stations. At the end of the lesson, stop the music to signal that the children are to stop what they are doing and listen for instructions.

- Station 1—Pumpkin Bowling: This activity is explained earlier in this chapter on pages 84-86. Refer there for a more detailed explanation of how to organize this fun way to practice climbing and rolling.
- Station 2—Roll the Pumpkin: Rolling, a precursor to throwing, is usually practiced through rolling a ball among children sitting in a circle on the floor.

Children delight in rolling a large pumpkin instead of a ball across the circle to each other. Refer to pages 106-107 in *Moving With a Purpose* (McCall and Craft 2000) if you require a more detailed explanation of this activity.

As children roll the pumpkins, sing the following chant together:

I have an orange pumpkin
As round as it can be
I'll roll it over to you
And you roll it over to me

- Station 3—Pumpkin Gutter Ball: In the original game of Gutter Ball, children roll tennis balls down a continuously sloping chute made from vinyl gutters. Change the game to Pumpkin Gutter Ball by having children roll miniature pumpkins, gourds, or orange plastic balls, instead of tennis balls, down the gutter chute. This activity is a fun way to practice visual tracking along with grasping and releasing. Pumpkin Gutter Ball is a variation of Carl the Construction Worker described on pages 96-98 in chapter 8 of this book. The original Gutter Ball is described on pages 70-71 in *Moving With a Purpose* (McCall and Craft 2000).
- Station 4—Move and Seek: Hide miniature pumpkins under a few of the several cones or small boxes you arrange at the far end of the activity area. Children run (or hop, jump, or walk backward) across the room to the cones, and lift each cone in turn, seeking to discover which cones have pumpkins concealed underneath. Once they have discovered pumpkins, the children carry them back to the starting point, then go back to search for more pumpkins. This activity prompts children to really concentrate and remember the position of objects. The original Move and Seek activity is described on pages 83-84 in *Moving With a Purpose* (McCall and Craft 2000).
- Station 5—Pumpkin Obstacle Course: This is a variation of the Jumping the Hurdles activity in chapter 6 on pages 74-76 of this book. Add pumpkins so children are challenged to step, jump, or leap over and move around pumpkins as they negotiate their way through the obstacle course. This activity is a delightful way to practice moving around objects while learning the concepts of spatial relationships. Place a pumpkin in the middle of a path so the child must walk around it. Or place pumpkins side by side in a line to make hurdles for children to jump over.

Adaptations

Refer to the original explanation of each activity in other sections of this book or in *Moving With a Purpose* (McCall and Craft 2000) for adaptations.

Variations

Use pretend pumpkins, not real ones as suggested earlier, for the following additional station activities.

- Pumpkin Throw: Cut a sheet of plywood to create the outline of a huge, three-foot by three-foot (1 m) pumpkin. Also cut a large mouth, a nose, and two eyes out of the plywood pumpkin and paint the whole thing orange. Use this plywood pumpkin as a target with a barrier, such as a folded mat, in front of the target. Young children enjoy standing close to the pumpkin target and trying to hit it with soft throwing objects. Older children may like the challenge of standing back from the target to practice throwing for accuracy as they try to toss soft objects through the pumpkin's mouth, nose, or eyes. Regardless of skill level, throwing at a pumpkin target is a fun way to practice object control.
- Stickers on the Pumpkin: This is a variation of Apples in the Tree described in chapter 9 on page 106 of this book. Cut a four-foot (1 m) pumpkin out of orange paper and laminate it. Tape it to a wall high enough that the tallest child will have to stand on tiptoes to reach its top. Let children perform various locomotor movements up to the pumpkin, place pumpkin adhesive stickers on the huge pumpkin, and return to the starting point. You may also want to use leaves cut from paper or any objects associated with autumn to decorate the pumpkin. Alternately, challenge children to place the stickers up as high as they can or down as low as they can to give them practice balancing. It's reusable if you wash off the stickers soon after using them.
- Singing Pumpkin: Purchase a battery-operated toy that moves and makes noise when the sensor detects motion. Drape an orange cloth, decorated like a pumpkin, over it. Hang the motion piece just beyond the children's reach. They will clap and clap and clap to make the pumpkin wiggle.

Changing the Space

- In a small space, set up only one station with a few children playing at a time.
- In a large space, set up several stations and provide extra adult supervision.
- Outdoors, conduct the stations much the same as indoors.

chapter 8

Gutter Games

Mr. Howitt had just finished replacing his house gutters. As he carried the remnant pieces of gutter to his garage, he thought, What a shame to waste these extra lengths. He picked up a tennis ball and let it roll the length of the gutter. This got him thinking about how he might use these gutters in his job teaching physical education to young children. Soon he had developed three highly original activities to help children learn object control.

SO YOU THOUGHT GUTTERS were just for houses? These unbreakable, lightweight vinyl channels are great for designing a variety of motor activities for children, and they're easy to store, too! Vinyl gutters can be found at most hardware stores, and they can be nested so that several gutters can be stored vertically in a corner or secured overhead to a beam, out of the reach of children. This chapter shows three very different ways these gutters can be used to help children increase lung capacity and develop skills as diverse as tracking and spatial awareness.

Air Ball

Cardiovascular endurance

This motivating activity, with its incredibly easy setup, will have children inhaling deeply and exhaling forcefully for minutes at a time. Children enjoy the instant gratification of seeing their breath move an object.

Overview

Introduce deep breathing and breath control by having children blow table tennis balls, toy plastic cars, or other lightweight objects along the gutter.

Goals for Children

- Develop breath control
- Increase lung capacity

Equipment

- One gutter, typically six feet (2 m) in length
- A lightweight object to move with breath
- A desk, table, or stack of mats at children's waist height

Equipment Tips

Use a table tennis ball, plastic golf ball, featherweight plastic toy car or other miniature toy on wheels, or whatever is at hand for children to blow along the gutter. Gutters are relatively inexpensive, but can often be obtained for free. Ask around to learn if someone has extra gutters to donate after a house construction project.

Preparation

Although the ends of gutters are not especially sharp, they can be made safer by filing the edges to round them or covering the edges with duct tape. Place the gutter on a table at children's waist height.

Instructions

1. Two children can play by standing at each end of the gutter and blowing an object back and forth to each other. One child can play by standing at one end of the gutter and blowing the object to the other end. Place a plastic bin or tape a paper cup to the end of the gutter so that the object will fall into it.
2. Place the object in the gutter and have the children blow away!

Adaptations

This activity may be excellent for children with noncommunicable pulmonary conditions for which breathing exercises are recommended. It is a fun way to incorporate the breathing exercises in a game played with others. A child unable to walk or stand independently may use adapted equipment such as a gait trainer or mobile prone stander (see figure 1.1 on page 10).

To aid children who have difficulty blowing forcefully, prop up one end of the gutter as it rests on the tabletop so the ball will roll more easily down the incline. Allow children who are unable to blow to use their fingers to push the object.

Variation

Increase the length of the gutter or the weight of the object to be blown. Now the children must blow harder to get the object to its destination.

Changing the Space

This activity requires little space and few props so it can be set up successfully almost anywhere.

Follow the Brightly Lit Road

Motor planning • Spatial relationships • Locomotor skills

Children learn to move with confidence as they follow a path of lights in a darkened room. This is a thrilling activity for young children that helps them practice depth perception.

Overview

Make a maze to stimulate sensory awareness by placing strands of white or multicolored lights inside the channels of the gutters. Create the effect of a lighted airport runway at night and have the children follow the path.

Goals for Children

- Enhance depth perception and sensory awareness
- Develop locomotor skills

Equipment

- A minimum of eight pieces of varying length vinyl gutters (paired equal lengths) or tubing to create a two-sided zigzag path. The length of the path will depend on the space available. Provide at least four turns to create a path that is fun for children.
- Mats, blocks, or other equipment to safely prop the gutters approximately one to one and a half feet high (PVC piping works as an alternative to gutters)
- A string of lights to place inside the gutters
- Flashlights

Equipment Tips

- Ask colleagues and friends for any remnants of vinyl gutters they may have in a garage. Determine whether a parent works in construction and may be able to donate excess gutter lengths. Otherwise, purchase gutters or PVC piping at a hardware store.
- Purchase Christmas lights after the holiday at a discount. Alternatively, purchase inexpensive strings of lights at discount chain stores. They sell lights for many different holidays and even summer outdoor string lights of different themes.

Preparation

Assemble available gutter sections to make two parallel tracks at least 20 feet (7 m) in length that zigzag if space permits. Create a two-foot-wide (1 m) path in the middle through which the children can run. Use bins, boxes, or other objects to elevate the gutters one

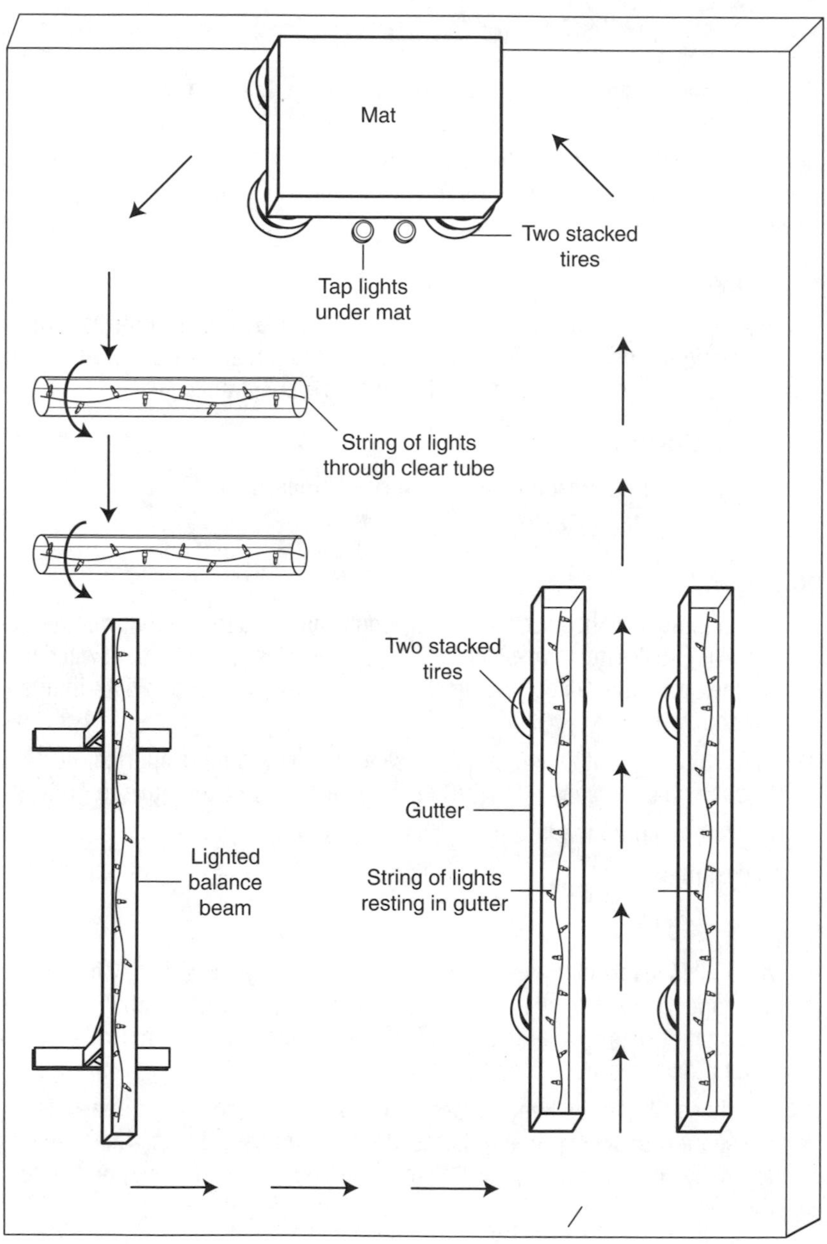

to one and a half feet off the ground so children are able to see the lights. Lay the string of lights along the middle of the gutters. If using PVC piping instead of gutters, wrap the lights around the piping. File gutter ends or cover them with duct tape.

Instructions

1. As an introduction to this activity, simply pull down the shades or turn off one set of lights in the room.
2. As the children become accustomed to following the path, darken the room further. Use your judgment as to how much you can darken the room. If the children feel safe and comfortable, reduce the lighting in the room until it is completely dark. Children may follow the lighted path using only a flashlight.

Adaptations

Use adapted equipment such as gait trainers or mobile prone standers to assist children who are unable to walk independently to negotiate the path. If any children are nonambulatory but able to crawl, lower the lighted course to the floor so that they can see the lights. Have all the children crawl through the course.

Variations

- Create varied theme paths. If using a string of white lights, have the children pretend they are airplanes landing at night. Encourage them to simulate the noise and movement of an airplane as they approach the runway.
- Purchase strings of lighting in novelty shapes such as pumpkins, bunnies, or horses. Prompt the children to imitate the novelty shapes as they move along the lighted zigzag path.
- If you have access to clear tubing at least three inches (8 cm) in diameter, thread a string of lights through the tube. Place the tubes across one of the paths to form lighted hurdles over which children can jump or step as they follow the brightly lit road.
- Use several colors of lights throughout the path and assign a movement to each color: jump in the red section, tiptoe in the white section, and crawl in the blue section.
- Use strings of lights with different themes such as stars, pumpkins, moons, and suns to designate different movements.

Changing the Space

- In a small space, limit the length of the lighted path and the number of children using it at one time. You can also create paths using tap lights, the small battery-operated lights that turn on when the dome is pressed. Tap lights are available in a variety of shapes such as circles, stars, and moons. One variation is to set up one area where children can crawl through a cave to get to the next set of gutters. They touch a tap light, turning it on and illuminating the cave. It is fun and encourages problem solving.

- In a large space, you can increase the size of the lighted path and the number of children participating.
- This activity may work outdoors if there is a tent or other darkened area or if parents simply want to try it with their own children at night.

Carl the Construction Worker

Motor planning • Object control

Carl the Construction Worker is a fun variation of Gutter Ball, found in *Moving With a Purpose* (McCall and Craft 2000, 70). Children love to pretend they are the popular cartoon character Bob the Builder in this game. The gutter now becomes the cement chute, and each ball becomes cement traveling down the chute. Add construction hats for the children to wear to accentuate the theme.

Overview

Gutter Ball, and now Carl the Construction Worker, is a novel way to create a pathway through your space. Use several gutters cut to various lengths and connected with vinyl elbow joints. Position the gutters at a gradual incline from a child's shoulder height to floor level so that balls in the chute will roll downhill. The children will be ready to practice grasping, releasing, and catching along with developing a sense of timing and the ability to visually track the rolling balls. This is also an outstanding activity for promoting speech among children as they imitate Bob, Wendy, Scoop, and the gang from Bob the Builder shouting, "Can we do it? Yes, we can!"

Goals for Children

- Develop grasp and release
- Develop visual tracking
- Develop anticipatory timing

Equipment

- Vinyl gutters of various lengths
- Elbow joints to connect gutters
- Stands to support gutters such as boxes, crates, mats, and blocks, or create homemade PVC stands as shown in the earlier photos
- Tennis balls, plastic balls, or other small balls to roll inside the gutters
- Two boxes for collecting the balls—one at the top and one at the bottom of the chute
- Construction hats, whether real or toy, borrowed from the classroom activity center or purchased at a dollar store

Equipment Tip

Refer to the activity Air Ball on page 91 for gutter equipment tips.

Preparation

Create a continuously sloping chute using gutters and elbow joints placed on supports. Allow at least six feet (2 m) of gutter for every four children. Decorate the room with posters and pictures of construction workers and equipment to promote dramatic play and language (McCall and Craft 2000).

Instructions

1. Children place tennis balls in the top of the gutter chute and let them roll downhill, attempting to stop and grab them before they reach the collection box at the bottom.
2. Check that children are periodically emptying the tennis balls from the collection box back into the dispensing box at the beginning of the chute. Prompt children to place balls in the gutter, stop rolling balls with their hands to create a blockage, and push any balls that became stuck in the corners. Also physically assist children who may be just learning to grasp and release (McCall and Craft 2000).

Adaptations

This activity is wonderful for including children with widely differing abilities. Children who are nonambulatory can be positioned in mobile prone standers, gait trainers, or wheelchairs in front of a gutter section. The adapted equipment allows their hands to be free to drop balls into the chute and block or push rolling balls. From this position they can actively participate in the game alongside their peers.

Children with visual impairments can also participate in this activity. Add bells or beepers inside the balls to make noise when rolled. Use brightly colored balls to assist children with partial sight (McCall and Craft 2000).

Variations

- Create a water park, using water instead of tennis balls. Children scoop and pour water down the gutters into a collection bin. It is great to play outdoors on a hot day while wearing bathing suits.
- Write names on the tennis balls. Children will dig in the dispensing box to find a ball with a specific name on it. Younger children can work on recognizing the initial letter of a name, and older children can try to read each name.

Changing the Space

- In small spaces, run the gutters throughout the building or house from one room to the next. Children delight in seeing gutters run across their living room, down the hall, and into the kitchen.
- In large spaces, set up one giant construction site or two to three smaller sites.
- The game can be played outdoors in the same manner as indoors or played as the water park variations.

chapter 9

Move and Match Activities

Mrs. Chermak wants to plan her movement lessons for the week, but is unsure about the space that will be available to her. Her usual teaching stations may not be accessible. The activity room is under construction. The weather forecast calls for rain throughout the week so the playground may not be an option. She realizes that she needs to be ready to teach in a classroom, if need be. She wants to teach activities that will help children learn locomotor skills as well as reinforce the cognitive concepts they are learning in the classroom. She also needs activities that use minimal equipment that can be easily carried from room to room and stored in a small space. Finally, she wants activities that can be conducted either in a small classroom or out on the playground if it is not raining.

THE MOVE AND MATCH ACTIVITIES in this chapter may be a great option for Mrs. Chermak and other teachers who have limited space, need to carry their equipment with them, want to teach locomotor skills along with cognitive concepts, and want their young children to have fun as they learn. The eight Move and Match activities in this chapter emphasize learning cognitive and motor skills and de-emphasize competition. The rules are simple and the variations are endless. In all of the activities children move enthusiastically from one end of the play space to the other; take or leave a requested toy, theme card, or other object; and then return to the starting point.

Move and Match activities are great motivators for young children to practice walking, running, jumping, hopping, skipping, and other locomotor skills as they go from point A to point B and back again. Use more sophisticated variations of these activities to motivate older children to practice ice skating, roller skating, walking on stilts, or other locomotor sport skills. These activities also lay the foundation for playing relay activities at an older age.

TEACHING MOVE AND MATCH ACTIVITIES

The eight Move and Match activities in this chapter are presented in a progression. The first two, Smiley Face and Apples in the Tree, teach children to move from point A to point B and back. These activities offer an enjoyable way to learn the concept of returning to the teacher. You may want to use these activities regularly with three- and four-year-olds. Typically developing five- and six-year-olds need to play it only once or twice at the beginning of the school year to learn the routine of returning to the teacher. The next six activities build on these first two, adding further instruction, more complicated movements, and more advanced cognitive skills.

When conducting Move and Match activities, keep children continuously active. They should be coming and going between points A and B continuously and in a staggered fashion. Either have all the children go at once or, if there are many children, have them go in small groups. As soon as each child returns from point B to point A, give him or her the next item to match. Do not ask children to wait until everyone has finished their first match before beginning their second match. With this arrangement, no child needs to wait for a turn. It will also be easier to inconspicuously redirect a child who has made an incorrect match when no other children are standing idly by.

Two activities do not lend themselves to children coming and going continuously. In both Pizza and Let's Make a Meal, all children are to match the one item that the teacher is holding, so everyone must complete one match before giving children the next match. If waiting is unavoidable, involve children who are waiting by asking them to count until all the other children have returned or chant a cheer as the others move. Consider introducing group competition against the clock. A large-faced wrestling clock is ideal, but a kitchen timer will also work. Be sure to set the time so that all children finish just before the buzzer sounds. Do not identify winners and losers or those who finished in first, second, and third place. Keep the Move and Match activity fun for children of all abilities by avoiding child-versus-child competition.

In a big, bold way, identify where the children are to start and finish each activity. Perhaps post a picture of a popular cartoon character on the wall or place a large mat on the floor to mark the starting and finishing areas. Avoid asking young children to sit on lines or to sit in formation. Divide large groups of children into smaller groups and clearly designate a separate spot for each small group to start and finish. Periodically ask the children where they are to finish the activity. Be proactive when prompting them to remember, and avoid reprimanding them when they forget where to go.

When first playing these activities, make the distance between the two points reasonably short so children have an easy time staying focused on their destination. Young children may become distracted and change their direction midway across the activity area if distances are too far.

Use these activities to enable children to practice a variety of locomotor skills. Initially ask the children only to run to point B and back. Following are various locomotor skills the students can use to move from point A to point B:

- To increase the challenge, ask the children to jump until they reach point B, then run back to point A. Tougher challenges are to jump to point B and then gallop back, or to walk backward to point B and then hop back. You can also add scooters for children to sit on and push to their destination, or have the children roller-skate back and forth, if they are sufficiently skilled to do so safely.
- Create obstacles in the path around which more skilled children must negotiate. Add obstacles to jump over using pieces of foam or pool noodles. Add whatever safe objects you have available such as plastic cones or cardboard blocks to create obstacles for the children to go around. Change the obstacles each time you play the activity to keep the activity fresh and motivating.
- Add tunnels to crawl through using fabric tunnels or chairs draped with cloth.

You can also use a Move and Match activity to teach one or two young children to climb stairs. This is especially applicable to children who may be over three years of age but not yet climbing stairs as a result of a developmental delay. Designate the bottom of the stairs as point A. Prompt the child to climb the stairs to point B. Here the child selects a matching card from among those you have scattered on the landing at point B. The child then climbs back down the stairs carrying the card. Be sure to carefully spot children just learning to climb stairs. Also, provide a way for the child to carry the card in a pocket or on a bracelet so that the hands are free for holding the handrail.

Once children understand the concept of moving from point A to point B and back to A presented in the first two activities, add the cognitive challenge of matching. In the remaining Move and Match activities, beginning on page 108, the children are asked to move to point B, find a match for a selected item, and return it to point A. Include cognitive tasks to enhance and stimulate movement activities. The children will be asking to play the Move and Match activities again and again. Try to incorporate key concepts highlighted that particular week in the classroom or acknowledge a season, holiday, or special event. Introduce various themes that young children love. The possibilities are endless!

MORE TIPS FOR MOVE AND MATCH ACTIVITIES

Move and Match activities are wonderful for teaching language, speech, and cognitive concepts because young children can build their vocabularies as they move and match. Teachers of English as a Second Language (ESL) who are looking for a fun way to teach English vocabulary will find these activities very helpful. Speech therapists seeking playful ways to have children practice speech articulation and fluency will find that these activities motivate children to vocalize the name of each object they are matching.

Classroom teachers who want novel and active ways to practice cognitive concepts may also find these activities particularly useful. One example is teaching children the concepts and names of shapes. Children gradually understand the concepts of circle, square, and triangle as they find and retrieve each of these shapes, matching them with the example the teacher is holding. These Move and Match activities promote conversations about shapes. As children talk about these concepts, they begin to understand them better.

Laminate or cover activity theme cards with contact paper so they are durable enough to use from year to year. Enlist parents or other volunteers to help cut, color, and laminate activity materials. Inquire at your school or a local teacher center as to whether there is a library of pattern-making dies that you can use to quickly cut multiple copies of different shapes, which will save you many hours of work.

Varying the cognitive challenge of these activities based on the ability of each child playing is easy. Consider the Move and Match Pizza variation called Highway Patrol as an example. Ask the very young or less advanced child to find any picture of a car and bring it to you. Ask the older, more advanced child to find a picture of a red car and bring it to you. Cut a variety of photos showing cars with background scenery from magazine ads and use them for theme cards. As children hand you the cards, ask each child something about the photo such as, "How many wheels can you see?" or, "How many doors can you see?" Simply change the question asked to vary the challenge to suit each child's needs. Remember to only ask a few questions so you can maintain the quick flow of the activity.

Children with diverse special needs have played these activities successfully over the years. Consider the following suggestions as you plan how to include children with special needs in each game:

- For children unable to walk independently, use adapted equipment such as gait trainers or mobile prone standers to assist them in moving from point A to point B and back. If a child is nonambulatory but able to crawl, have all the children crawl between points.

- For children with limited vision, use large theme cards or stickers that have bright colors and high contrast to increase their visibility. Provide a guide for children to assist them with orientation and mobility as they move between points. Play the game alongside a wall so children with limited vision can trail their hands along the wall to guide them between points A and B. Provide an oral commentary so that children can follow what is occurring even if they cannot see others playing the game.
- For children who are deaf or hearing impaired, sign and say the instructions.
- For children with autism, put the word as well as the picture on each card. Some children with classic autism are able to understand printed words more easily than images.
- For children with intellectual delays, simplify the tasks. Children who learn slowly may need many opportunities for practice to learn to travel between points A and B. Focus on having them master this concept before expecting them to make a proper match.
- For children with emotional difficulties—and all children—do not introduce any competition into the activities. Stress each child's individual accomplishments without making comparisons to other children. Keep all children actively involved in the game so there are no spectators to watch and make judgments about others' performances.

Additional adaptations are provided within some of the activities. We encourage you to read all of the adaptations in this chapter to gather more ideas for fully and meaningfully including children with special needs in each game. Have fun together as everyone learns to move and match!

Smiley Face

Locomotor skills • Object, color, and shape recognition

This game is a low-cost, simple way to work with young children of widely different cognitive and motor abilities. For the least skilled children, it is an opportunity to learn the concept of going from here to there and back again. For more advanced children, it is an opportunity to practice locomotor skills. This game enables everyone to play together joyfully while practicing at their individual ability levels.

Overview

In this simple game, each child gets a smiley face sticker at the starting point, runs to the other side of the space, and places the sticker on a huge smiley face posted on the wall. Each child then returns to the starting point to get another sticker and repeat the activity.

Goals for Children

- Learn to move between two points
- Develop fine motor coordination by handling stickers
- Learn to return to the teacher

Equipment

- One giant smiley face taped to the wall
- One package of smiley face stickers, or at least four stickers per child
- A colorful means of marking point A, such as a poster of a favorite cartoon character

Equipment Tips

You can purchase the giant smiley face at a party source store, or you can make your own by cutting a large circle out of yellow paper, then drawing a smiley face on it. Laminate or cover the smiley face with contact paper for durability. If you remove the stickers from the laminated surface within a few hours, you can reuse the giant smiley face again and again. If you choose to leave the stickers in place on the smiley face, plan to make a new giant smiley face that is not laminated every time you play the game.

Sheets with a thousand stickers can be purchased at a dollar store. If your budget is low, shop for inexpensive stickers, then vary the game's theme from Smiley Face to whatever fits with the stickers you buy.

Preparation

Preparation for most Move and Match activities is minimal. Prepare for the Smiley Face game by simply taping a cartoon poster on the wall at point A and taping the giant smiley face to the wall at point B.

Instructions

1. Gather the children at point A, the designated starting and ending spot. Give them each one sticker.
2. Point to the smiley face hanging on the wall at point B. Explain that the children are to cover it with smiles!
3. Tell the children that when they are all smiling at you, you will say go! They are to run down and place their sticker on the smiley face and then run back. Depending on the number of children playing, they can go either individually or all together.

4. Continue the game until all the stickers are gone or the smiley face is covered.
5. As a conclusion, you can hang the smiley face in a special place where the children can view it over the next day or week.

Adaptations

Learning to remain with the teacher or return to the teacher when asked to do so can be challenging to learn, especially for very young children and those with attention difficulties related to autism or attention-deficit/hyperactivity disorder (ADHD). This game is also helpful in motivating children who may want to just sit down once they get to point B. This and other basic Move and Match activities provide fun ways to practice the concept of going away from and then returning to the teacher. Refer to the chapter introduction for additional suggestions.

Variations

Vary the theme to fit the season, holiday, or stickers that you have available.

- Draw a giant paper flowerpot with flower stems in it and ask children to put flower stickers on the ends of the stems.
- Draw a giant pumpkin and cover it with pumpkin stickers.
- Draw a giant cartoon character and cover it with stickers of the same character.
- Draw a giant dinosaur and cover it with dinosaur stickers.
- Draw a giant horse or unicorn and cover it with matching stickers.
- Draw a giant food basket and cover it with stickers of fruits and vegetables.

For older children or with smaller groups, cut a giant circle, a square, and a triangle from construction paper. Tape the three shapes side by side on the wall at point B. Give each child a round, square, or triangular sticker and ask him or her to place the sticker on its corresponding shape. Children now have to also distinguish among shapes in the activity.

Changing the Space

- In a small space, this game works well for children who are first learning how to play Move and Match activities. The short distance between the two points means that children are less likely to become distracted and forget where they are to go. Use different locomotor patterns such as hopping, crawling, and jumping in smaller spaces.
- In a large space, this game works well with children who are already familiar with the activity and can move between the two points without losing their focus. Increase the distance to give children extra practice with the locomotor skill they are using to move between points. If you increase the distance between points to more than 25 feet (8 m), this activity can help develop cardiovascular endurance.
- This game works very well outdoors as long as there is a wall, fence, or other vertical surface on which to mount the giant smiley face.

Apples in the Tree

Locomotor skills • Object, color, and shape recognition • Stability

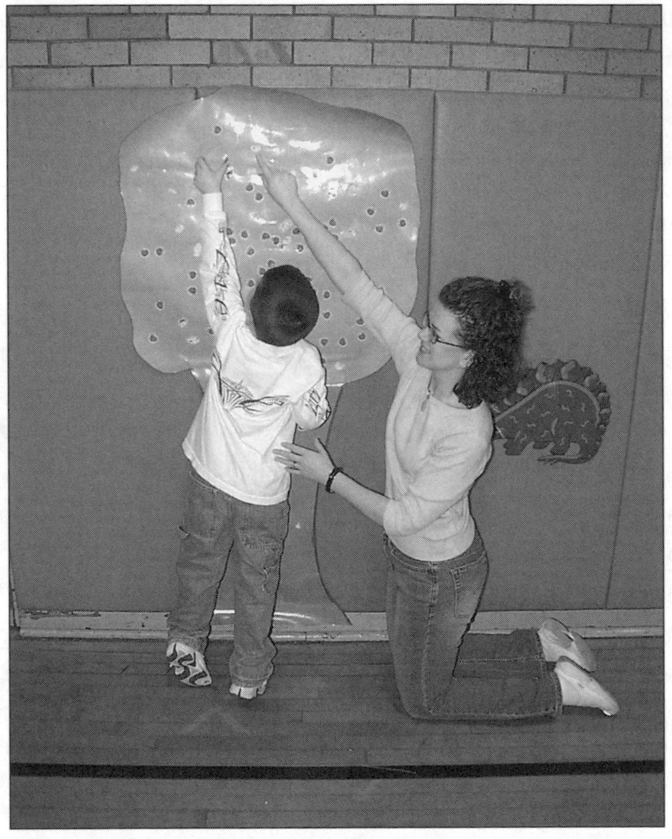

This activity is a motivating way to help children learn the vocabulary of high and low as they stretch and bend.

Overview

Apples in the Tree is more difficult than Smiley Face because it challenges children to reach up high on their tiptoes and squat down low as they place apple stickers on a huge picture of an apple tree.

Goals for Children

- Learn to move between two points
- Develop fine motor coordination by handling stickers
- Listen for a key word
- Develop static balance while squatting and on tiptoes

Equipment

- One four-foot paper apple tree
- One package of apple stickers, or at least four stickers per child
- A colorful means of marking point A

Equipment Tip

The four-foot apple tree can be cut from construction paper or traced on rolled paper, then laminated for durability.

Preparation

Tape the giant apple tree to the wall in a position high enough that the children will need to stand on their tiptoes to reach the treetop.

Instructions

1. The instructions for this game are similar to those of Smiley Face, with the substitution of apple stickers for smiley face stickers and an apple tree for a giant smiley face. Begin by gathering the children at point A and giving each child an apple sticker.
2. Point to the apple tree taped to the wall at point B. Explain that the children are to cover it with apples!
3. Tell the children that when you say the word *apple,* they are to run to the tree, place their sticker on it, and run back. Surprise and tease them by sometimes saying a word other than *apple.*
4. Continue the game until all the stickers are gone or the tree is covered with apple stickers. Encourage children to put stickers at the treetop so they need to balance on tiptoes and at the bottom of the trunk so they need to balance while squatting.
5. Hang the tree in a special place where the children can view it regularly.

Adaptations

Place a sticker in both hands of any children who may have limited use of one hand, perhaps due to cerebral palsy or amputation. Encourage children to reach up high with their more functional limbs while also making sure that they reach as high as possible with limbs that have less mobility.

Variation

Print *apple* in large letters under the tree. Ask, "What sound do you hear at the beginning of the word *apple*?" Ask more advanced children, "What letter makes that sound?" If a child's name begins with the letter *A*, ask her to place a sticker on the word that begins with the first letter of her name.

Draw a country scene on a length of rolled paper, complete with the sun in the sky, a birdhouse on a pole, a bird nest in a tree, and worms on the grass. Challenge children to stretch and squat as they place bird stickers on the birdhouse, in the nest, and on the ground near the worms.

Changing the Space

Refer to suggestions in Smiley Face on page 105.

Pizza

Locomotor skills • Object, color, and shape recognition

Most young children love pizza with the colorful toppings of red tomatoes, brown mushrooms, green peppers, pink shrimp, and yellow pineapple chunks. Use this familiar food as a fun way to teach color identification as children select toppings to place on their plain pizza slices.

Overview

Children move from point A to point B and back, gathering toppings for their pizza slices that match the topping examples you display. They particularly enjoy sticking each topping on the laminated pizza slice, creating the finished product of a fully loaded pizza.

Goals for Children

- Develop locomotor movements
- Develop ability to match pictures

Equipment

- One picture card of a plain pizza slice per child, plus one for demonstration
- Six picture cards of toppings per pizza slice
- Tape to place on the back of each pizza topping card
- A colorful means of marking point A

Equipment Tip

To make pizza toppings and slices, cut construction paper in the desired shapes and then draw and color them to resemble a plain pizza slice and topping of cheese, pepperoni, pineapple, olives, sausage, peppers, mushrooms, or broccoli. Laminate toppings and slices for durability.

Preparation

Colorfully mark point A, perhaps by taping a motivating cartoon poster on the wall. Spread pizza toppings on the floor, tape them to a wall, or place them on a low table or stacked mats at point B.

Instructions

1. Gather the children at point A, the designated starting and ending spot. Show and ask the children to name each pizza topping and its color as you demonstrate how to place toppings on your plain pizza slice.
2. Give each child a slice of plain pizza and tell them in a funny, overly dramatic way that all the pizza toppings are waiting for the children at point B.
3. Hold up a picture of a topping. The children are to move to point B, find the topping that matches what you are holding, place it on their pizza slice, and bring the slice back to point A. As the game progresses, vary the instructions for moving from point A to point B and back. One time ask children to walk backward. Another time ask them to gallop, and so on.
4. Stop briefly after each round to do a pizza check to make sure the children have selected the correct topping. If a child has made an incorrect match, simply ask the child to go back and try again. Phrase the request so that you emphasize your desire for the topping, rather than the fact that the child has made a mistake. Sometimes you may want to invite the child to bring a friend along to help.
5. Continue the game until all the children have placed all the toppings on their pizza slices.
6. A silly conclusion is to pretend to eat the delicious pizza everyone has just made. Another option is to place a sign reading "Pizza Oven" on an overturned box or a hard plastic tunnel. Conclude the game with everyone placing their pizza slices inside the oven as they leave the activity room.

Adaptations

To accommodate children who have special needs that limit their ability to bend over and pick up something from the floor, place the pizza toppings on a waist-high table or other elevated surface so they can easily place the toppings on the slice.

Some children may have difficulty grasping or may need to use their hands to hold a gait trainer. Attach string to the pizza slice so they can carry it on their arm as a bracelet.

Variations

- Vary the locomotor challenge. Ask children to run down and jump back, or hop down and gallop back. For a highly skilled group of children, add obstacles around which they must negotiate.
- Increase the number of task requests. Have children perform two or three tasks at points B, C, and D before returning to point A.
- Teach a variety of cognitive concepts through Move and Match activities. Some children may be ready to practice letter recognition using alphabet cards. Similarly, they can practice name recognition using name cards. Challenge older children to spell words by collecting individual

letter cards at point B and assembling the letter cards into words back at point A. Provide practice in writing sentences by collecting cards with words on them at point B and assembling the words into sentences back at point A. Match numbered playing cards to practice addition or subtraction. Challenge older children to select three cards at point B that, when added together, will equal a specified sum. As an example, a child might select the playing cards 3, 5, and 8 to total the requested sum of 16.

- Shape Up is an activity that is played much the same as Pizza. Children are to match shapes in addition to colors, making the task a bit more complicated. You need a variety of shapes and colors, such as 15 circles, 15 squares, 15 rectangles, and 15 triangles, laminated for durability; a plastic bin in which to place the shapes; and a colorful means of marking point A. Begin by holding up each colored shape you will be using and listen as the children identify its shape *and* color. Explain that the children are to select a shape from among the squares, rectangles, triangles, and circles on display at point B that is the same color and shape as the shape you are holding and then bring it back to point A. Ask questions such as, "How many sides does a square have?"

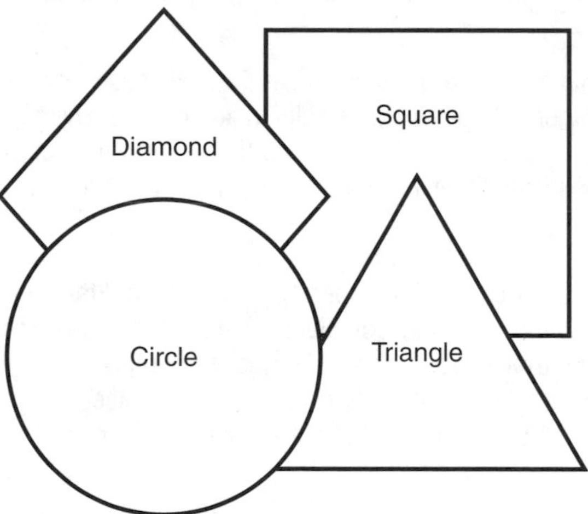

- Highway Patrol capitalizes on young children's keen interest in cars, trucks, buses, trains, and other vehicles. This variation of the Pizza activity teaches object identification. Print out many pictures of vehicles from clip art on a computer, cut them out, and tape or laminate them to index cards. Provide at least one card of each vehicle per child, plus one card of each vehicle for demonstration. Playing with 10 children would require 11 fire truck cards, 11 bus cards, 11 train cards, 11 police car cards, and so forth. You will also need a plastic bin in which to place the cards and a colorful means of marking point A. Follow the same instructions as those for Pizza, substituting pictures of vehicles for pictures of pizza toppings. Children move from point A to point B, find the vehicle card that matches the card that the teacher is holding, and bring it back to point A, where they put it in a bin. Continue until all the cards have been matched. Ask children to name the vehicle pictured on the card. Ask more advanced children to identify the initial sound or letter of the vehicle name. Only ask a few questions to maintain the quick flow of the activity.

Changing the Space

- In a small space, limit the number of children playing and reduce the distance between point A and point B. Slow children's movements by asking them to crawl, roll, tiptoe, or walk backward instead of run.
- This activity can be played as described in a large space or outdoors.

Supermarket Sweep

Locomotor skills • Object, color, and shape recognition

Children love to imitate adults shopping! Here is a clever way to have children practice locomotor skills while learning to match a grocery item to its picture. By adding a zigzag path between points A and B, you help them also learn to maneuver as they go.

Overview

Children move from point A to point B and back, grocery shopping for the toy fruit or vegetable that matches their picture card. Supermarket Sweep is more challenging than Pizza because now each child is looking for a different item, rather than the same item as everyone else.

Goals for Children

- Develop locomotor movements
- Identify and match foods

Equipment

- A large variety of plastic or stuffed fruit and vegetable toys
- Laminated picture cards cut or drawn to resemble each of the plastic or stuffed fruits and vegetables. Provide at least four foods and matching cards per child.
- A plastic bin to hold the food
- A colorful means of marking point A
- A poster of fruits and vegetables, if available

Equipment Tip

Plastic or stuffed fruit and vegetable toys are typically available at dollar stores, through Constructive Playthings (www.cptoys.com), or through donations.

Preparation

Make picture cards. Colorfully mark point A and spread the plastic or stuffed fruit and vegetable toys at point B. If available, also hang the poster of fruits and vegetables at point B.

Instructions

1. The instructions are similar to those of the preceding Pizza activity. Give each child a picture card of a fruit or vegetable. Explain that they are going grocery shopping for the fruits and vegetables waiting for them at the store at point B.
2. Children are to find the plastic or stuffed food that matches the card they are carrying and bring the food and card back to point A. Each child then places the food in the bin and gives the card to you. As each child returns with the food and card, immediately give the child the next card. Children do not have to wait until every child has found the first food before starting again. If time permits, ask children to name the food they collected and perhaps describe something about it. Again, be sure to maintain the quick flow of the activity so children do not have to wait for the next card.
3. If children are having difficulty finding the match, use the poster as a visual cue to prompt them.
4. When all the food has been gathered, reverse the process by asking the children to return the food to the store and restock the shelves.

Adaptation

For children who may have difficulty holding a card, place the card in a paper bag with handles. Children can hold the bag in their hand or wear it over their wrist while shopping. Once they find the food match, they can use the bag to carry the food and the card back to point A.

Variation

Use balance boards, lengths of board, cones and rope, or any safe items to create a zigzag path for children to travel as they go from point A to point B. Have children return to point A along the outside of the zigzag path to keep a safe flow of traffic.

Changing the Space

Refer to suggestions in other Move and Match activities.

Going to the Zoo

Locomotor skills • Object, color, and shape recognition

Children love to cuddle stuffed animals. This activity, a modification of Supermarket Sweep, gives them the chance to hug and squeeze stuffed animals as they learn to move and match.

Overview

Children move to and from the zoo, selecting and retrieving the stuffed animals that match the picture cards they are holding.

Goals for Children

- Develop locomotor movements
- Identify and match animals

Equipment

- A large variety of small stuffed animals
- Laminated picture cards cut or drawn to resemble each of the stuffed animals
- A plastic bin or pool large enough to hold all of the stuffed animals
- A colorful means of marking point A

Equipment Tip

Stuffed animals can often be had for the asking from parents and community members. Call for donations of stuffed animals, and you may find you are given more than you need. Once you have a sizable number, you can use them again and again for motivation in many different activities.

Preparation

Colorfully mark point A and place stuffed animals in the zoo at point B.

Instructions

1. The instructions are similar to those for the earlier Pizza activity. Begin the activity by giving each child a picture card of an animal. Tell them that all the stuffed animals that match their cards are waiting for them in the zoo at point B.
2. The children are to find the stuffed animal that matches the animal pictured on the card they are carrying and bring the stuffed animal and card back to point A. Each child then places the stuffed animal in the bin and gives the card to you. Give the child another animal card immediately so he or she can return to the zoo to find the next match.
3. After all the animals have been collected, ask the children to return the stuffed animals to the zoo and begin again.

Adaptations

Refer to the suggestions at the beginning of the chapter under "More Tips for Move and Match Activities."

Variation

Add obstacles between points A and B so children practice stepping over, going around, and moving through objects as they travel to the zoo and back again.

Ask children about the initial consonant sounds of the animal names. Questions can include, "What letter does *zebra* begin with?" "What is the sound at the beginning of the word *zebra*?" "How many parts to the word *zebra* do you hear?" We recommend only asking a few questions to maintain the quick flow of the movement activity.

Changing the Space

Refer to suggestions in other Move and Match activities.

Let's Make a Meal

Locomotor skills • Object, color, and shape recognition

This activity is a fun, novel, and active way to teach nutrition concepts. Children move back and forth between points, filling their paper plates with pictures of healthy foods.

Overview

Children move from point A to point B, select the requested food, and then return to point A. Unlike the preceding activities, this activity requires the children to remember the requested food without the aid of a theme card in their hands for comparison. It also challenges the children's abilities to grasp and place small objects.

Goals for Children

- Develop locomotor movements
- Use a pincer grasp
- Match pictures

Equipment

- One paper plate per child, plus one for demonstration
- Five laminated menu item cards per plate, cut or drawn
- A colorful means of marking point A
- Velcro strips
- A table or folded mats for menu items at point B.

Equipment Tips

Line drawings of food items are available as clip art on most computers. Just print out the number and size of the pictures you need. The small amount of Velcro needed for this activity can be purchased in strips at fabric stores or discount department stores.

Preparation

Adhere five 2-inch (5 cm) squares of Velcro loops to the eating surface of each plate. Then adhere a 2-inch (5 cm) square of Velcro hooks to the back of each menu item card. Now the Velcro hooks on the menu item cards can stick to the Velcro loops on the plate.

Menu items could be pictures of healthy breakfast foods such as orange juice, unsweetened cereal, a piece of fresh fruit, toast, and a glass of milk.

Instructions

1. The instructions are similar to those for the earlier Pizza activity. Give each child a paper plate. Explain that they are going to fill their plates with pictures of healthy breakfast foods waiting for them on the table at point B.
2. Have the children leave their plates at point A and move to point B to find the food picture that matches the food picture you show them. They bring the food picture they find back to their dinner plate at point A and attach it to the plate using Velcro. Ask children to name the food as they attach it to the plates.
3. After everyone has "taken a helping" of each food, sit down together and pretend to eat the meal. Then continue the activity in reverse, putting each of the menu items back at point B.

Adaptation

Some children will need to use their hands to hold a walker or other adapted equipment for assistance as they move between points. Enable them to carry the food picture with them by attaching it to a Velcro belt placed around the child or on the walker.

Variations

- This is a great activity to do just before Thanksgiving with everyone pretending to dish up Thanksgiving dinner with plates full of cooked turkey, bread, corn on the cob, carrots, and a glass of milk.
- Make pictures of foods for healthy lunches, dinners, or snacks. Plan five foods for each meal, creating several copies of each food picture. If you make food pictures for several meals, you will develop an extensive library of food pictures. You can use all of these food pictures for the next variation. Ask children to name foods as they select them.

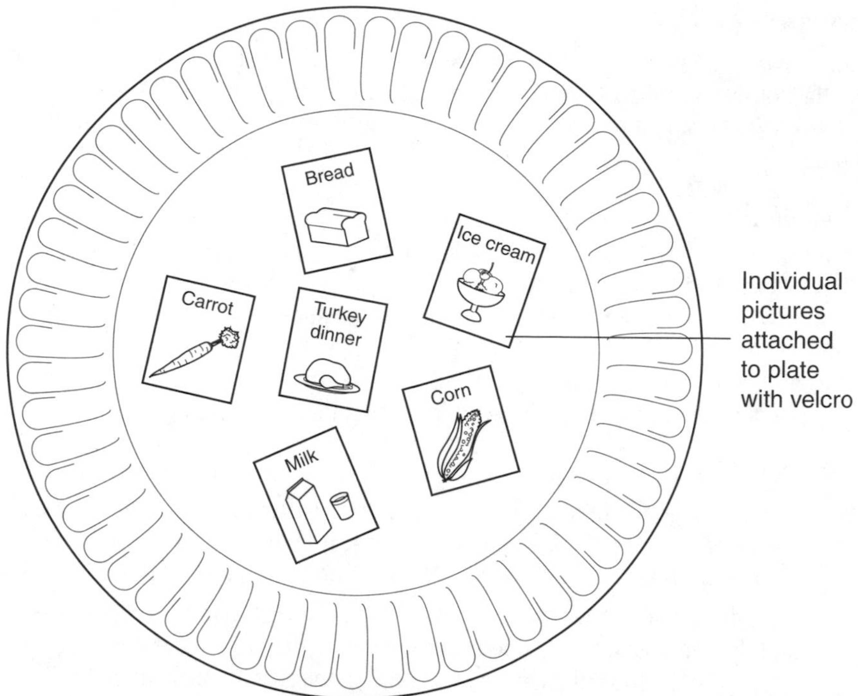

- Teach older children to identify food groups from the food pyramid. Instead of simply showing them a food item and asking them to retrieve identical food pictures from point B, name a food group and ask them to select foods that are in the food group. Ask, "Can you find a food that is a grain and bring it back?" Children may select and return with toast, cereal, or rice from among the many varied food pictures displayed at point B. Instead of placing the food picture on dinner plates, consider asking children to attach the selected food to a large poster of the food pyramid. Adhere small Velcro squares onto the pyramid so the food pictures can be attached to it. If funds permit, you may want to purchase a flannel board and up to 100 felt pictures of food from Constructive Playthings at www.cptoys.com.
- Challenge children to select healthy foods for a meal from among a variety of both healthy and unhealthy food theme cards displayed. Ask them to select a healthy breakfast, teaching them to choose food pictures of unsweetened cereal, fruit juice, and toast, but bypass the food pictures of donut, soda, and french fries.

Changing the Space

Refer to suggestions in other Move and Match activities.

Mitten Match

Locomotor skills • Object, color, and shape recognition

Young children's days are filled with crayoning, finger painting, cutting with scissors, and drawing. Here is a way to give them practice with the fine motor skill of the pincer grasp while being physically active. Children enjoy this activity because they imitate an adult task.

Overview

Children practice matching colors and using the pincer grasp as they imitate adults hanging mittens to dry on the clothesline.

Goals for Children

- Develop locomotor movements
- Use a pincer grasp

Equipment

- A large variety of laminated paper mittens. Provide one mitten of each color per child, plus one for demonstration. Playing with 10 children would require 11 of each color mitten (red, blue, purple, green, yellow, and so forth)
- One bag of spring clothespins so there is at least one clothespin per mitten
- A clothesline strung horizontally across the space, long enough to hold all of the mittens
- Eyebolts or another means of attaching the clothesline to a wall or other solid support
- A playhouse placed next to the clothesline to create the feeling of a real backyard (optional)
- A colorful means of marking point A

Equipment Tips

Clothespins are for sale at dollar stores. Be sure to buy the spring clothespins that have two parts that you squeeze to open, rather than the push-on kind, because you want children to use the pincer grasp to open the clothespins.

Preparation

String the clothesline at the children's eye level. Secure the rope so that it can withstand the weight of children pressing on it. Pin five or six mittens to the clothesline in advance as examples. Pin several extra clothespins on the line for children to use for hanging their mittens.

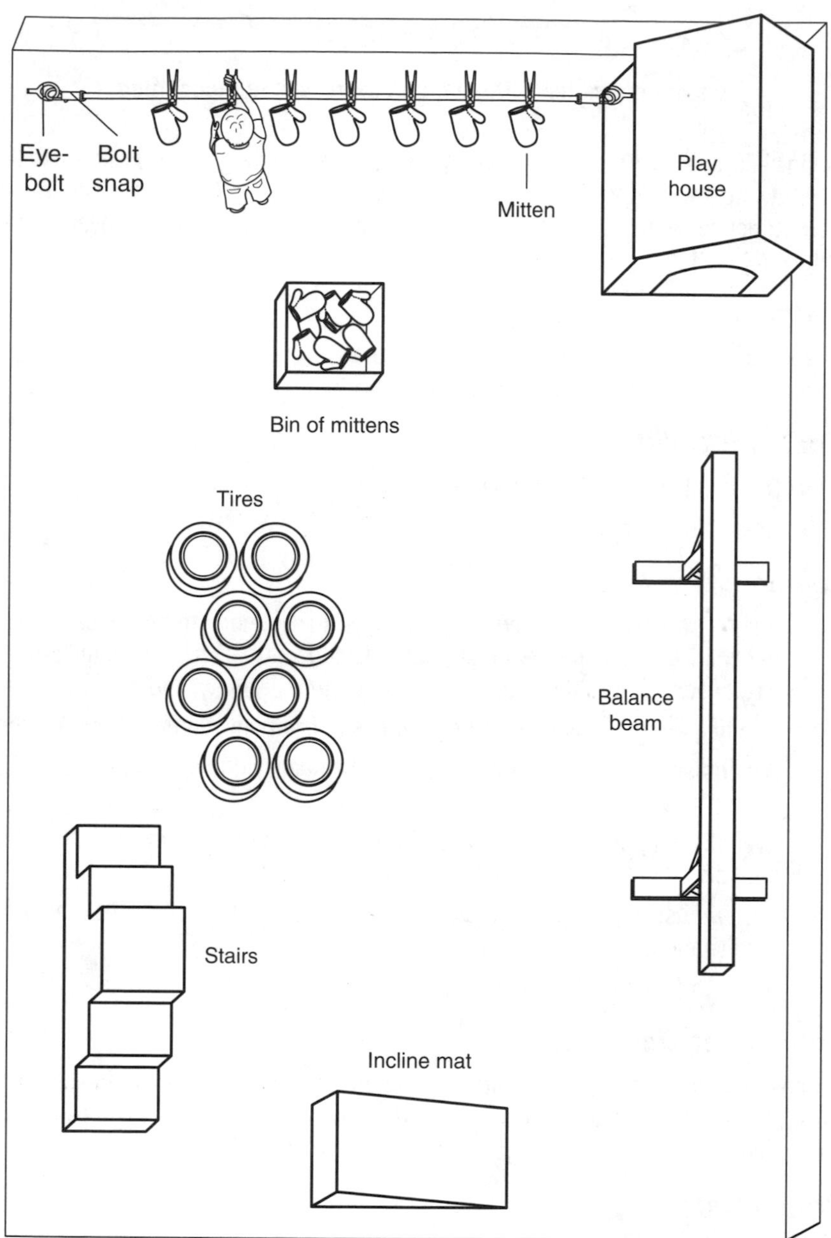

Instructions

1. The instructions are similar to those for the earlier Pizza activity. To introduce the activity, hold up each color mitten you will be using and listen as the chil-

dren identify the color. Explain that all the mittens that match the color you are showing are waiting for them at point B.

2. On cue, ask the children to go to point B. Here the children are to select a mitten that matches the color you are holding from among the mittens on display. Then the children are to press together the two parts of the spring clothespin to open it and pin the mitten on the clothesline to dry. The children then return to point A.
3. After all the mittens have been pinned up to dry on the clothesline, ask the children to unpin the mittens, place them back at point B, and begin again.

Adaptations

With children who are unable to use the pincer grasp because of physical limitations, one option is to substitute push-on clothespins for the kind with a spring. Another option is to attach a strip of Velcro hooks over a short section of the clothesline. Attach Velcro loops to the backs of the mittens. Now children who are unable to grasp can simply pat the mittens onto the clothesline with the Velcro.

Variations

- To increase the challenge, use plastic clothespins of different colors and specify both the color of the mitten and the color of the clothespin that children are to select.
- Increase the challenge by incorporating floor beams, low balance beams, and low steps into the activity. Children move from point A to point B by walking on the balance beams and up and down the steps. They next select mittens and pin them on the clothesline. Children then circle back to point A by walking across additional balance beams.

Changing the Space

- In a small space with stairs, provide practice climbing up and down the stairs. Ask the children to climb the stairs from point A at the bottom to point B at the top, walk over to the clothesline and hang the mittens, then climb back down to point A.
- In a large space or outdoors, add more obstacles for children to negotiate as they move between points.

Sport Ball

Locomotor skills • Object, color, and shape recognition

Children are drawn to this activity because it uses a variety of balls from different sports. This activity is sure to appeal to children who fancy themselves as sport buffs. They are thrilled when they make a whole sport ball by matching its two halves.

Overview

Children move and match the two halves of sport balls in this activity. Children carry one half of the sport ball from point A to point B. They then use the half in their hands for comparison as they look for the matching half already taped to the wall. Once they find a match, they tape the half in their hand next to the one on the wall to create whole sport balls.

Goals for Children

- Develop locomotor skills
- Practice object identification

Equipment

- Laminated cards depicting images of a large variety of sport balls (at least four balls per child), each cut in half
- A colorful means of marking point A

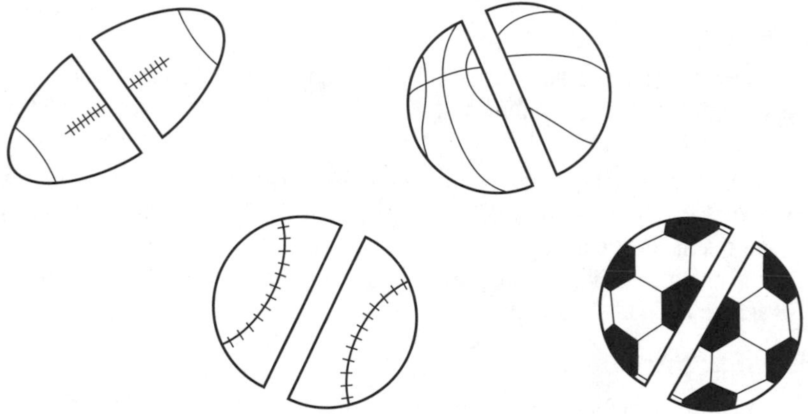

Equipment Tip

Instead of drawing your own sport balls, purchase an inexpensive party banner with various sport balls on it. Cut out an example of each type of ball, and you are done!

Preparation

Cut out, color, and laminate the shapes of a variety of sports balls from paper. Use basketballs, soccer balls, footballs, baseballs, tennis balls, or golf balls. Once the pictures are laminated, cut each sport ball in half so children can try to match the two halves during the activity.

Instructions

1. Draw the children's attention to the many and varied sport balls displayed as wholes at point B. The balls can be spread on the floor, taped to a wall, or placed on a large low table or on stacked mats.

2. Dramatically take one half of every sport ball away so that only one half of each ball remains displayed at point B. Bring the halves you removed from point B back to point A. Ask each child to pick up a half on your cue.
3. On the word *go,* children carry the sport ball half you gave them from point A to point B, where they find its match. They then tape the half in their hand on the wall next to the half at point B to create a whole ball. Finally, they leave the whole balls at point B and return to point A.
4. Continue the activity until all the sport ball halves have been made whole. Repeat if time permits.

Adaptation

The tape on the back of each paper sport ball half usually enables children who are unable to grasp to hold the cards as they move to point B.

Variations

- Another inexpensive way to present a sport theme is to purchase novelty paper plates that depict sport themes. Many plates have food dividers so they fit together in only one position. In this variation, show children a sport plate, such as the skateboarder plate, then ask the children to find its match among the plates displayed at point B. Children move from point A to B, find the plate's match, and bring it back to point A. They then put one plate on its match, rotating the plates until both fit snuggly together.
- Match the Valentine is another variation found in McCall and Craft (2000, 79-80).

Changing the Space

Refer to suggestions in other Move and Match activities.

Part III

Programs for Purposeful Play

Part III offers a wealth of movement activities and curriculum resources for those interested in teaching children to cycle safely and make wise fitness and nutrition choices. We also introduce Lucy, the 55-foot (20 m) inflatable whale. Learn how you can build Lucy the whale and conduct movement activities within and around her to add unbelievable excitement to your program. Finally, we share 10 special events you can organize and conduct to promote your program. Hold several of these special events throughout the year so that parents and key decision makers are informed about, and will be enthusiastic in their support of, your movement program.

chapter 10

Let's Cycle Safely!

Mr. Smith pauses for a moment during the movement lesson to scan the room. He smiles as he watches the children pedaling through the bike village he created. Mr. Smith recalls that only 10 months earlier Jared was just beginning to pedal a tricycle independently. Now Jared proudly pedals his bicycle with training wheels. Steven, who has cerebral palsy, was using foot straps because he lacked the strength and coordination to hold his feet on the pedals. Now he confidently pedals his tricycle all by himself—strap free! Spencer presented the greatest challenge because he can move his head and arms only a few inches independently. He now can sit securely on an adapted tricycle and be pulled by an adult. Spencer delights in being able to cycle alongside his peers. Mr. Smith recalls the many teaching suggestions, lesson plans, and resources that enabled him to help each of these children find success in cycling.

"*CAN YOU TEACH MY CHILD* to ride?" tops the list of the most frequently asked questions by parents of preschool or primary movement program children. Learning to ride a tricycle and later a bicycle are rites of passage for many young learners. Learning to cycle safely is also important. This chapter contains many ideas that will encourage you to begin or enhance the tricycle and bicycle riding aspect of your movement program. Help children safely enjoy the fun and cardiovascular benefits of cycling!

The first part of this chapter has hints for starting a cycling program and offers suggestions for teaching children to ride tricycles and bicycles. It continues with lesson plan ideas for creating exciting pedaling environments that encourage safe cycling practices, and then discusses organizing a special tricycle riding event. The second part of this chapter offers strategies for purchasing low-cost helmets and teaching cycle safety using community resources and curriculum kits. Although we discuss tricycles throughout this chapter, you can easily substitute bicycle riding in each activity for those children with more advanced skills.

STARTING A CYCLING PROGRAM

If you would like to provide an opportunity for the children in your care to practice cycling, this section offers a few tips on getting started.

- **Assess.** Start by assessing the equipment and space available to you, along with the children's cycling ability levels.
- **Acquire equipment**. If your center or school is able to accept donations, this is a wonderful way to obtain the needed bicycles and tricycles to offer a cycling program. Check with your program administrator to determine policies on donations. Ask colleagues and friends who are parents of children who might be outgrowing their small tricycles and bicycles. Don't forget to make the rounds of yard and garage sales for inexpensive used cycles. Should your budget allow the purchase of cycles, consider purchasing an adapted tricycle or bicycle from Rifton or a Dura Trike from Flaghouse. Both companies sell adapted cycles that are known for their durability. We list addresses for both companies in the "Resources" section at the end of this chapter.
- **Inspect for safety.** Whether you acquire new or used cycles, be sure to inspect all equipment regularly to ensure that it is safe to use.
- **Provide helmets.** Provide a bike helmet for every child who is riding a cycle. Later in the chapter you will read where you can purchase helmets for $5 each. Ask service community groups to donate helmets if your program or community families do not have the funds to purchase them.
- **Organize the cycling area.** Locate a large space with a firm, smooth surface on which children can cycle. Provide one cycle per child, with the cycle fitted to each child's size and skill level. Don't discourage a small child from climbing on a large bike, but suggest a smaller tricycle before the child heads out into cycling traffic. Remove clutter, including excess cycles, from the space so only equipment needed for the cycling lesson is available. Teach children to cycle in only one direction. Create a parking lot where the children should return all cycles not in use. Prompt the children to put their cycles away on their own in a designated parking spot.
- **Plan to prevent chaos.** Have tasks for children to do while they are cycling. We strongly recommend using theme cards, such as Valentine cards, for children to gather and deliver as they cycle. Use these theme cards to keep children focused and to redirect children who are beginning to be off task. We offer lesson plan ideas using theme cards later in this chapter.

This child enjoys riding a tricycle while learning the importance of wearing a helmet.

- **Supervise and evaluate**. Supervise children as they ride. Two adults may be necessary with many young riders. One adult can facilitate the theme card tasks while the other helps beginning riders learn how to cycle. Revise the lesson until all children are experiencing joy and purpose as they cycle.

LEARNING TO CYCLE

Most children are riding tricycles by age three, and then later begin riding bicycles. Many children can learn how to ride a tricycle without any instruction. They have watched other children do it and are now eager to do it themselves. They merely need the opportunity to try. Other children will need a few prompts to start, such as the following:

- Sit on the seat.
- Hold onto the handlebars.

- Keep your feet on the pedals.
- Push down on the pedal.
- Turn the handlebar to turn the tricycle.

Some children will need even further instruction. The following section offers ideas for children who are physically capable of pedaling a tricycle, but are having a little difficulty coordinating the movements. Remember to supervise children at all times when they are riding tricycles, and be sure they wear helmets.

Foot Straps

Use foot straps for children who cannot keep their feet on the pedals. You can purchase straps from adapted tricycle companies listed in the "Resources" section at the end of this chapter. A low-cost alternative is to make foot straps by attaching Velcro straps to the pedals. *Caution:* Do not secure the feet of children capable of pedaling fast. With their feet strapped in, they will not be able to catch themselves if they turn a corner too fast or tip for any other reason.

Ankle or Waist Weights

Children who are having difficulty keeping their feet on the pedals may be aided by placing a three-pound (2 kg) weight around each ankle. Also consider using weights around the waist of a child who tends to shift around on the tricycle seat. Attach 2 three-pound (2 kg) weights together using the weights' Velcro straps, and then place the weighted belt around the child's waist. Always consult with a physical therapist and the child's parent before placing weights on a child. The child may have a medical condition unknown to you that would make using weights unwise.

Steering Bar

A steering bar, or push bar, is a long handle extending from the back of a tricycle. It allows you to grasp the bar and steer the tricycle without having to bend over to reach it. Steering bars can save your back from stress and strain during a cycling lesson (see figure 10.1). Tricycles with steering bars attached to the back are available both in toy stores and through sport catalogs listed in the "Resources" section at the end of this chapter. A low-cost alternative to purchasing a steering bar is to weld one onto the back of the bike.

Photo courtesy of Kettler International.

Figure 10.1 Use a steering bar to assist in pushing your students who are learning to cycle.

Pull Rope

Another way to help children move and steer a tricycle is to loop a short jump rope around the handlebar of the tricycle. Pull on both ends of the rope to move the child on the tricycle, or on either end to help steer. This gives beginners a chance to feel their legs cycling up and down so they can begin to understand the pedaling motion. You can even pull two or three children at one time to help move them one step closer to independence!

Pushing Legs

By placing your hands on a child's legs and pushing down, you can physically assist the child through the pedaling motion. This strategy helps beginners understand what to do when told to push down on the pedals.

Transition Bicycles

Training wheels help children avoid falling off their bicycles during the difficult transition from a tricycle to a bicycle. You can further reduce the frustration of the transition by first having children ride a transition bike, which has 10-inch (25 cm) wheels, training wheels, and no foot pedal brakes. The 10-inch-wheel bike does not go as fast as the larger 12- to 14-inch-wheel (30 to 35 cm) bikes, so it is a good intermediate step between the slower tricycle and larger, faster bicycles. Typically the 10-inch-wheel (25 cm) bike does not have foot pedal brakes so children do not get into the habit of intermittently braking and pedaling, adopting a stop-start-stop-start motion instead of pedaling continuously. After gaining experience with a transition bike, children will more easily move up to the larger bike and use foot pedal brakes more skillfully. Typical children may transition from the 10-inch-wheel (25 cm) bike to the 12- to 14-inch-wheel (30 to 35 cm) bike in two to four weeks with regular practice.

TRICYCLE ADAPTATIONS FOR CHILDREN WITH SPECIAL NEEDS

Many children with special needs (e.g., limited strength, balance, or movement) can learn to ride tricycles and bicycles independently using a variety of commercially available equipment adaptations (McCall and Craft 2000, 41). Refer to the Rifton Equipment and Flaghouse Special Populations catalogs listed in the "Resources" section at the end of this chapter to order adapted bicycles.

Hand-Propelled Tricycles

Use hand-propelled tricycles with children who are nonambulatory and have use of their upper bodies. With the Rock N' Roll Cycle sold by Rifton, riders pull and push a bar forward and back with their hands to propel the tricycle. In the hand crank style, riders propel the tricycle with their hands using chest-height handles that rotate in the same manner as foot pedals. A platform provides a footrest. Use hand- or foot-driven tricycles with children who have some, but limited, movement in their arms or legs. These cycles are propelled by either traditional foot pedals, hand cranks, or both.

Seat Belts and Backrests

Children who need additional support to sit upright on the tricycle can use tricycles with backrests, also known as sissy bars. Children with limited trunk strength and stability may need a seat belt in addition to a backrest for added support.

Seat belts will keep children from sliding forward on the tricycle seat. Typically, the optimum pedaling position is with children's hips, knees, and ankles each flexed at 90 degrees as they sit on the tricycle or bicycle. The Rifton and Flaghouse Special Populations catalogs have many more cycle models designed to meet specific needs. All of these cycles are quite expensive, but accessories to make adaptations can be purchased separately at a lower cost. A fat wheel tricycle with a sloping backrest might be an inexpensive alternative for some children. These tricycles can be purchased in toy stores.

Upright Handlebars

Handlebars that extend vertically will provide an easier grip for children who have difficulty grasping. This position is an alternative for children with cerebral palsy who may have difficulty rotating the forearm internally to grasp a conventional tricycle handlebar.

CYCLING LESSON PLANS

We want children to experience the joy of cycling in a safe environment, both at home and at school. For this reason, the safety education process should begin as soon as a child is introduced to wheeled recreational toys at the preschool level. Providing free play on available cycles in a motor area or playground is insufficient for quality instruction in cycling. Young children must be instructed in key concepts of safe play as they are learning to pedal. Introduce the first unit on tricycle riding and bike safety soon into the school year; then repeat it as the year progresses, adding new information each time.

The following section presents lesson plans and activities focused on teaching cycling skills and safety rules, and using cycling skills to develop cardiovascular endurance. The chapter concludes with information on options for purchasing low-cost bike helmets along with curriculum resources for teaching tricycle and bicycle safety.

Some children will learn cycling skills quickly and enjoy cycling as a result of their success. Others do not develop skills as quickly and may not want to ride at all unless they are encouraged. Creating the proper cycling environment—one that is safe, enjoyable, and appropriately challenging for all skill levels, as well as fun—has the best chance of satisfying all children as they cycle, regardless of their abilities. Create a miniature village in the cycling area, complete with a gas station, a post office, and a car wash. This village, made from readily available materials and lots of imagination, inspires the children as they cycle to perform tasks that adults normally perform in motor vehicles. Children excitedly pedal to the post office to mail letters, to the gas station to refuel, and through the car wash for the thrill of the experience. These ideas expand on the Tricycle Course activity presented in *Moving With a Purpose* (McCall and Craft 2000, 141).

Because children are often very excited about cycling lessons, you will want to contain their energy somewhat to avoid having lessons become chaotic. Here are some suggestions for maintaining a safe and orderly environment during any cycling lesson:

1. Begin with a fitness warm-up.
2. Introduce cycling safety concepts to the children by reading them a big book or having them view a short video.
3. Lead a physical activity to practice cycling skills.
4. Conclude with a cool-down and lesson summary.

These suggestions are addressed in the following two lesson plans designed to provide focus for children while they are pedaling. Modify the lesson plans presented here to suit the space and children in your program. Plan to include all children in the lesson, using adapted equipment as needed, so that everyone can enjoy cycling. Whether you are teaching a class of 2 or a class of 16 children, and whether you are teaching tricycle or bicycle riding, remember to keep it fun!

Lesson 1

This lesson is designed to teach tricycle or bicycle riding skills and to introduce cycling safety concepts. You may want to reinforce the cognitive concepts with theme cards. Ask children to cycle around the area and gather theme cards of a particular shape, color, food group, or letter from the theme cards displayed.

Warm-Up

Begin with a warm-up to music. Select a song from among the dictated music suggestions in chapter 3. Two warm-ups that emphasize body part identification or balancing, twisting, and turning in place are

- "Freeze" on Greg and Steve's CD *Kids in Motion* and
- "That's the Way It Goes" on Peter and Ellen Allard's CD *Sing It! Say It! Stamp It! Sway It!*

Safety Concepts

After the warm-up, introduce cycling safety concepts. Gather the children and view a brief video or read to them from a big book that teaches cycling safety. A favorite big book is *Berton on the Big Wheel*, a safe driving story available through the American Automobile Association (AAA) as described later in this chapter. Important tricycle and bicycle safety tips for cycling in the neighborhood are presented in "Cycling Safety Rules."

Cycling Safety Rules

Teaching cycling safety to young children is essential. Here are some examples of safety concepts that children should learn and follow:

- Always wear a helmet when riding a tricycle or bicycle.
- Wear sneakers, not sandals, when cycling.
- Only ride where adults are watching.
- Ride on sidewalks or in the yard; never ride in the street or down the driveway into the street.
- Watch for cars backing out of driveways.
- Stay away from behind a parked car in case an adult gets in and backs up the car without knowing you are there.
- Only go as fast as you can safely turn or stop.

Rules specific to riding a tricycle or bicycle during the movement lesson are as follows:

- Always wear a helmet when riding a tricycle or bicycle.
- Wear sneakers, not sandals, when riding to protect toes and feet.
- Only ride where adults are watching you.
- Only go as fast as you can safely turn or stop.

You may want to coordinate cycling safety lessons with classroom instruction so that you can concentrate on teaching cycling safety in active ways during movement lessons. Consider having the children view cycling safety videos, play the cycling safety maze board game, and do other sedentary activities from the *Play It Safe* curriculum kit (discussed later in this chapter) while they are in the classroom.

Following the introduction of cycling safety concepts, lead a physical activity such as You've Got Mail to practice cycling skills.

You've Got Mail

Cardiovascular endurance • Muscular strength and endurance
Motor planning • Object, color, and shape recognition
Spatial relationships

Young children love riding tricycles and bicycles. They also love to imitate adults. Ask children to mail letters, and they will have a great time doing what big people do. You've Got Mail combines both of these loves into a single activity.

Overview

In this activity you create a movement environment in which children perform the adult tasks of collecting and sending mail. This mail, referred to as theme cards, can be any of a number of items that relate to a specific theme. Children pedal around the activity area collecting theme card mail at the post office and delivering it to the mailbox.

Goals for Children

- Practice cycling skills
- Develop coordination
- Develop cardiovascular endurance
- Learn basic cycling safety concepts
- Learn cognitive concepts with theme cards

Equipment

- One tricycle or bicycle per child
- One bike helmet per child
- Five theme cards per child
- A box or stand to simulate a post office
- A toy mailbox
- CD of lively music
- CD player

Equipment Tips

Create a post office from a table, overturned box, or upside-down bin, adding a sign reading "Post Office." Create a mailbox from an old mailbox, bin, box, or small garbage can, with a sign reading "Mailbox."

Children ride around the activity area on their tricycles and bicycles, collecting mail from the post office and delivering it to the mailbox. Vary the lesson from day to day by changing the theme cards the children collect and deliver.

Preparation

Gather theme cards for children to mail. These can be old greeting cards, index cards with the children's names or pictures on them, or any theme cards you created for the Move and Match activities in chapter 9. Food theme cards can be made on 5 1/2-inch by 8-inch card stock, each with a photo, drawing, or wrapper of a food. Consider laminating your theme cards for durability so you can use them year after year in an assortment of activities.

Place the post office and mailbox at opposite ends of the activity area. Children will cycle between the two locations. Set the theme card mail on the post office table or box. Line the tricycles and bicycles along a wall before the children enter the activity area. This becomes the parking lot, the place where cycles are picked up and returned. Set out helmets, enough for every child, in a different part of the activity area. This avoids any potential confusion or accidents at the beginning of the activity because children are not putting on their helmets in the same area where others are starting to ride their cycles.

Instructions

1. After the warm-up and introduction of cycling safety concepts, gather the children together to sit as you describe the lesson activity. Show them the lineup of tricycles and bicycles. Tell them that during the activity each child will be free to select a cycle from among those lined up along the room or playground wall. Explain that this is the parking lot and that they are to return the cycles to this area when they finish. Tell them that they can change cycles whenever they wish, but they need to park their current cycles in the parking lot before getting other cycles. Also point out the area, away from the cycles,

where the bike helmets are and explain that every child must wear a helmet to participate.

2. Explain to the children that they are to pedal around the activity area collecting mail at the post office and delivering it to the mailbox.
3. Once you have explained the activity, invite the children to come to the helmet area to get their helmets. It may take up to five minutes to put helmets on all preschool children in a large class. Children in primary grades can put on their own helmets, although you will want to check them for a proper fit.
4. As soon as every child is wearing a helmet, begin the activity. Turn on the music to signal when it is time to start riding, and explain that they must stop riding when the music stops.
5. It is important to keep traffic flowing, always in a single direction, around the perimeter of the area. Explain to the children that they have the option of pedaling continuously around the perimeter or pedaling to the center where they may stop to perform a task related to the theme of the day. This helps maintain the safe flow of traffic. With the children now cycling, shift your focus to monitoring the safety of the activity. At least two adults are typically required for cycling lessons. One helps in the center of the activity area with the collecting and sending of mail. A second adult walks around and monitors the area giving the following reminders:

   - If your feet come off the pedals or your back wheel comes up off the floor when turning a corner, you are going too fast to be safe. Please slow down.
   - Ride, do not walk, around the perimeter.
   - Everyone needs to ride in the same direction.
   - If you are about to bump into someone in front of you, remember that you can go around the person.
   - Get off your cycle only to park it or help distribute mail.

   Younger children pedaling in a group need to learn to go in the same direction. Older children can also learn to pass on the left.
6. If you are monitoring the entire area, you will also need to offer individual assistance to children just learning to pedal a tricycle or bicycle. This might include pulling one or more children using tow ropes, putting on foot straps, and any other of the several teaching suggestions presented at the beginning of this chapter. Additional adults may be needed when working with children with significant special needs. Physical and occupational therapists may be able to provide therapy during cycling lessons.
7. If you are in the center of the activity area, encourage the children to ride to the post office to receive the theme card mail. Ask children to tell you what they are mailing to practice their language skills. Children take the mail and then pedal to the mailbox to deliver it. Remind them that they can grasp

the paper around the handlebar or slip it under their bottoms on the bike seat, then continue to pedal safely. At any time a child may choose to park his or her cycle and assist you in the post office distributing mail.

Adaptations

Refer to the earlier section titled "Tricycle Adaptations for Children With Special Needs" on page 130 for suggestions.

Variations

Use a different theme every time you teach a cycling lesson so that the activity remains fresh and novel. Theme cards can reflect holidays and seasons.

- Use Valentine's Day cards. You can usually buy these on sale after the holiday and save them for the next year.
- Cut paper shamrocks from green construction paper for a St. Patrick's Day theme.
- Cut pumpkins from orange construction paper for an autumn theme.
- Cut snowflakes from white construction paper for a winter theme.
- Cut colorful cards and send holiday greeting cards.
- Cut bunnies, chicks, and flowers from pastel construction paper for a spring theme.

Another way to increase the challenge is to ask children to gather only theme card mail of a particular shape, color, number, letter, or word from among the many theme card shapes, colors, numbers, or letters displayed. With elementary school children, select theme cards that reinforce language skills being taught in the classroom.

Changing the Space

This activity requires a large indoor space on a very low pile carpet or a bare floor. It can also be conducted outdoors on blacktop or cement surfaces.

Cool-Down and Lesson Summary

To end the lesson, turn off the music as a signal that it is time to stop pedaling. Remind the children to park the cycles and gather for a cool-down. A cool-down with young children is simply a time to sit down and rest. These young children are just learning the difference between vigorous exercise and rest. Ask them to feel the difference between their hearts beating fast during vigorous exercise and beating slower as they rest during the cool-down time. As children age, introduce slow stretching or other calming physical activities during the cool-down.

As children prepare to leave the activity area, play a soothing song, such as "As Quiet Can Be" on the Peter and Ellen Allard CD *Sing It! Say It! Stamp It! Sway It!* or sing the "So Long Until Tomorrow" song discussed in chapter 3 on page 29. Lead a brief review of cycling safety rules by asking questions such as, "What should you wear on your head when cycling?" or "Where do you park your cycles when you finish riding them?"

Lesson 2

This cycling lesson plan extends the post office and mailbox theme to create an entire miniature village complete with a gas station and a car wash. Encourage children to cycle continuously to increase their cardiovascular endurance.

Warm-Up

Begin with a warm-up to music. Refer to lesson 1 for warm-up suggestions.

Safety Concepts

Begin a discussion of cycling safety concepts by reading the big book *Play It Safe* that comes in the curriculum kit by the same name. Or read the book *Red Light, Green Light* by Margaret Wise Brown. The "Resources" section at the end of the chapter lists publication information for this book.

A Day in Bike Village

Cardiovascular endurance • Muscular strength and endurance
Motor planning • Object, color, and shape recognition
Spatial relationships

Here is a second activity that capitalizes on children's interest in imitating adult tasks. Use props to create buildings in a miniature village through which children ride their tricycles and bicycles.

Overview

Children cycle through a miniature village in this activity. In addition to the post office and mailbox described earlier in You've Got Mail, add a gas station, car wash, roads and obstacles, or whatever you and the children can imagine. Conduct the activity much like the preceding activity using theme card mail.

Goals for Children

- Develop cardiovascular endurance by cycling continuously for several minutes
- Develop motor planning by negotiating around obstacles
- Develop muscular strength and endurance

Equipment

- One tricycle or bicycle per child
- One bike helmet per child
- Gas station: overturned box with a rope attached, sign
- Car wash: spray bottle with water, string mop or crepe paper streamers, box fan, sign
- Roads and obstacles: road cones, mats, homemade street signs, metal mirror, or other safe obstacles
- Five theme cards per child
- CD of lively music
- CD player

Equipment Tips

Because young children have wonderful imaginations, you don't need realistic objects to represent the buildings in the village. Use whatever safe objects you have on hand.

Preparation

You will want to assemble the village prior to conducting the movement lesson. You can design and construct the village yourself or create it as a project in collaboration with the children and their classroom teacher. Once you have created the village, you may need only about 10 minutes to pull out the props and assemble the village the next time you teach this lesson.

- *Gas station:* Set up a gas station by attaching a rope or jump rope to a bin, crate, or upside-down box. Add a sign reading "Gas Station." Children love to stop at the gas station to fill up their "cars" before pedaling on their way. Give them the freedom to also get off their cycles to stand behind the gas pump and pump gas for classmates.
- *Car wash:* Set up an area where children pedal through the car wash. Use a spray bottle with water to spritz the children before they go through the car wash brushes. Create brushes by draping a string mop or crepe paper streamers from an overhead support. Add a fan at the end of the car wash to dry off the car. Children love this activity! Consider a safe way to suspend the brushes from the rim of a basketball net in a gymnasium or on a driveway. Be sure that the brushes will not fall onto the children if pulled. Position the

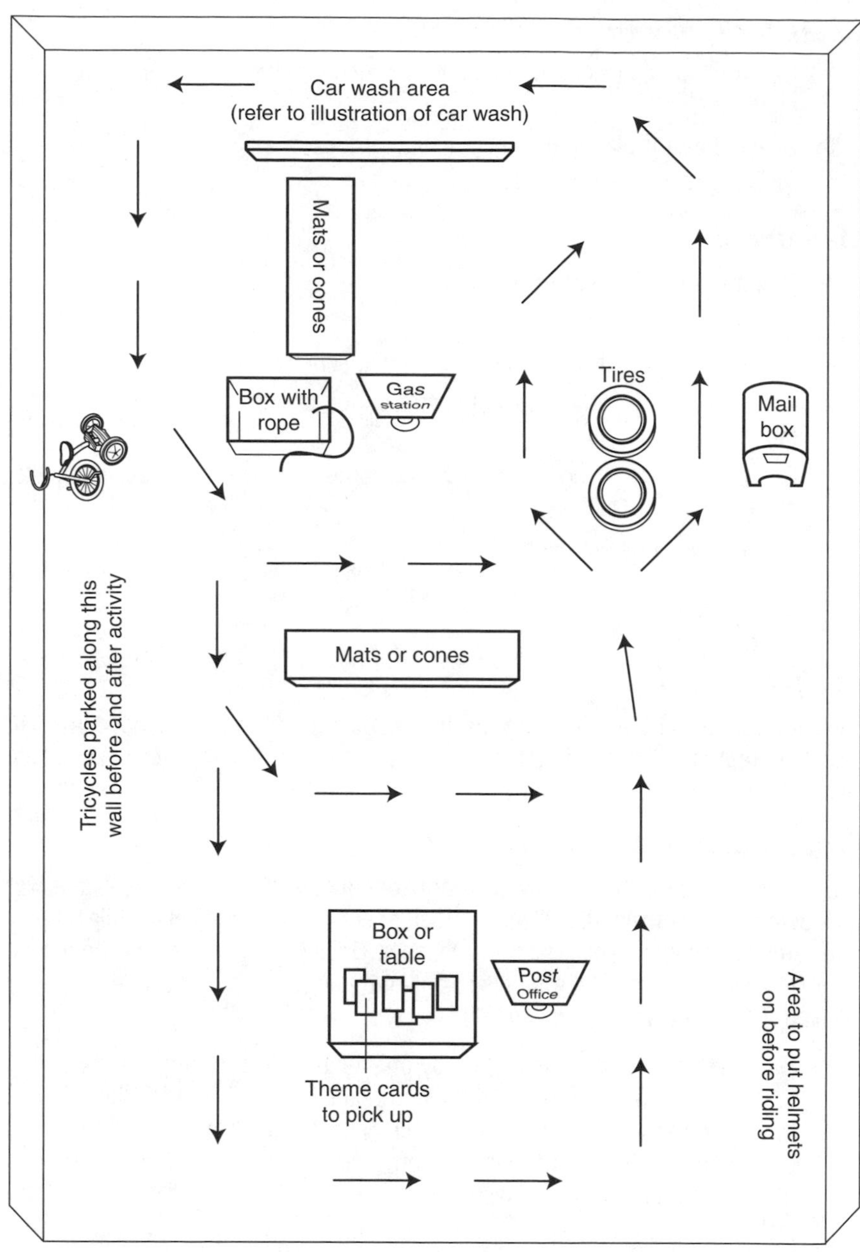

box fan on a table behind a barrier to designate safe boundaries. Remind children not to touch the fan. As always, provide adult supervision and designate safe boundaries. Look for ways to use bungee cords instead of ropes for attaching parts to the car wash. Bungee cords can be quick, inexpensive, and durable alternatives to ropes that can save you equipment setup and takedown time.

Add a sign with numbers that correspond to car wash services at the entrance to the car wash. This will give children who do not want to be sprayed with water a chance to decline that part. Selecting the number 0 means that the child only pedals through the brushes (crepe paper) and the blow-dry (fan). A child can request one spray of water by pointing to the number 1 on the sign, two sprays by pointing to the number 2, and so forth. Children love to use the sign, and they have fun while using numbers. Make the letters and numbers one inch high in boldface so children can easily read the sign without getting off their cycles.

0 = Brush and Blow Dry
1 = Rinse, Brush, and Dry
2 = Mini Wash, Brush, and Dry
3 = Big Wash, Brush, and Dry
4 = Super Wash, Brush, and Dry
5 = The Works

- *Roads and obstacles:* Whether inside or outdoors, set up obstacles such as road cones, mats, or homemade street signs around which children ride. If a playground surface permits, use chalk to draw streets along which the children can drive. These obstacles help children to remain aware of where they are riding, prevent groups of children from pedaling too fast, and require children to practice steering. If available, place a full-length metal mirror within the village so children can enjoy looking at themselves as they pedal by the mirror. This helps develop body image and also motivates youngsters. Position mirrors in a corner so children can pull off to the side without interfering with traffic flow.

Instructions

1. Introduce the activity and the instructions for safe cycling as explained in the preceding activity You've Got Mail. Put on the children's helmets, turn on the music, and let the cycling begin!
2. Provide at least two adults to monitor the activity: one adult at the post office or car wash and one walking the perimeter and helping children learn to cycle. More than two adults are needed if children with significant special needs are cycling. Allow children to assist the adult in distributing mail at the post office or allow them to distribute the mail themselves.
3. Try to conclude the activity when the excitement is still running high, before the children begin to lose interest. Often children will eagerly pedal for 20 to 25 minutes.

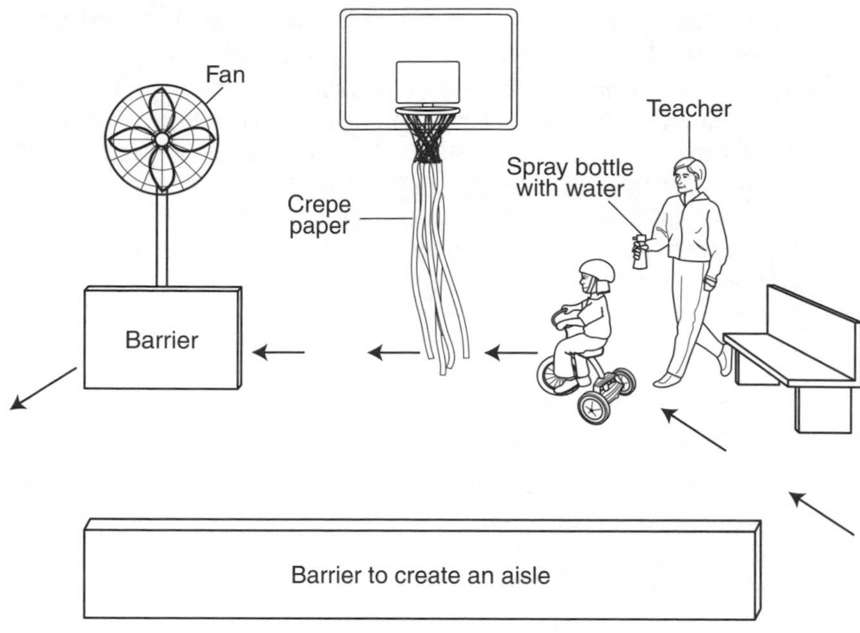

Adaptations

Refer to the earlier section titled "Tricycle Adaptations for Children With Special Needs"on page 130 for suggestions.

Variations

- Create sets of theme cards that reinforce cognitive concepts that children are learning in the classroom. Mark each card with a different letter of the alphabet and challenge primary school children to collect cards with each of the letters in their first names. Older children can collect theme cards with one word written on each card. Challenge them to collect all the words needed to write a complete sentence. Children may appreciate theme cards with pictures of different locations from across the country. They can pretend that they are sending postcards home from their travels across the country as they pedal.
- Ask beginning readers to collect cards that all have the same word on them. One child collects cards with the word *do* while other children collect cards with other simple words such as *go*, *at*, *the*, or *it*. Ask each child to find a different word so that they do not compete with each other for the same card.
- Consider using a lesson theme that reinforces identification of healthy foods as well as providing cardiovascular exercise. To conduct the activity Fruit Stand, convert the post office into a fruit stand, with appropriate signage.

Lay out food cards that depict healthy fruits and vegetables. Children cycle up to the fruit stand and receive a food card dispensed by an adult or child under adult supervision. Children place the cards on their seats and sit on them, and then pedal to the mailbox. Here they mail the food card through a slot labeled with various pictures and words of fruit and vegetables. Speech therapists may be eager to hand out the food cards because it presents the opportunity to work with each child on proper pronunciation as he or she requests and names the food on the card. You can also use food cards to practice color, number, and object recognition. Ask children to select food cards showing a fruit that is not red or the letter *A* in a name. Movement lessons provide wonderful opportunities to reinforce cognitive concepts.

Changing the Space

See "Changing the Space" in the You've Got Mail game on page 137 for suggestions.

Cool-Down and Lesson Summary

Turn off the music as the signal for children to gather for the cool-down and lesson summary. As they park their cycles, children often brush perspiration from their foreheads and say, "This was fun and I am hot," which is great because it means the children had a good workout.

Conduct the simple cool-down as explained in the You've Got Mail activity. Review cycling safety again. Award paper medallions on strings for children to wear at the completion of the cycling safety unit. It could say "I learned about bike safety today" with the date and a cartoon drawing of a child riding a bicycle.

The two activities You've Got Mail and A Day in Bike Village and the variation Fruit Stand can be done repeatedly over several days or periodically throughout the year. Use different theme cards each time you play the activity, but continually reinforce the same safety concepts. Within a short time, these little learners will realize the potential their tricycles and bicycles have for travel.

Ride for Life

In addition to cycling activities as part of your movement program, you can also conduct a Ride for Life event in your school or center to promote cycling safety and raise funds for heart disease research. Each year many physical educators across the United States lead students in physical activities to raise money to fund research on heart disease. Young children are often excluded from these events, however, because they do not yet have the requisite motor skills. Ride for Life is an alternative that gives young children a chance to participate in a special event while doing

something successfully that they love. Use this tricycle- and bicycle-riding event with young children of all ability levels. Promote the importance of cardiovascular fitness and safe play while children are pedaling.

Have regular tricycles, adapted tricycles, and any other necessary mobility equipment ready and waiting so every child can participate. A standard-sized gymnasium can easily accommodate 16 children cycling simultaneously. Place obstacles and stop signs at various locations around the space so children must negotiate their way through the course.

Ride for Life was initially developed as a joint effort with the Upstate New York Chapter of the American Heart Association (AHA) and the North Syracuse Early Education Program. The event has been used as a fund-raiser to support the AHA and to promote the AHA curriculum *Heart Power*, described in chapter 11. Typically, the AHA provides the *Heart Power* kit free of charge to programs that conduct AHA fund-raising events. Refer to chapter 13 for a more in-depth description of how you can conduct this truly special event that is ideal for children and for media coverage of your program.

EVERY CHILD NEEDS A BIKE HELMET

Everyone should wear a helmet whether riding a bicycle, riding a tricycle, riding as a passenger on a bicycle, roller skating, in-line skating, or skateboarding. Laws regarding wearing helmets vary from state to state, but it is always smart to wear a helmet. Facts about bicycle riding injuries are sobering (see "Facts on Cycling Injuries"). For questions regarding the helmet laws in your area, contact your local law enforcement agency, traffic safety bureau, or AAA. Further information is also available from the U.S. Consumer Product Safety Commission at their toll-free hotline 1-800-638-CPSC (2772).

Facts on Cycling Injuries

The highest rate of cycling injuries is in children who are 5 to 14 years old. In a single year more than 500,000 children have cycling injuries that are so serious as to require visits to physicians or hospital emergency rooms. The best way to protect children's brains and lives when cycling is to have them wear properly fitted bike helmets.

Adapted from American Automobile Association (AAA) Traffic Safety Department, 1988. *The teacher's guide to bicycle safety: Kindergarten—Grade 8* (Washington, DC: American Automobile Association).

If the children you teach are sharing helmets, remember to spray the inside of each helmet after every use to prevent the spread of head lice. Lemon Quat spray works well. See the "Resources" section at the end of this chapter for information on where to purchase Lemon Quat. Check with your program to follow any regulations regarding the use and storage of chemicals.

Let parents and guardians know how important it is that their young children wear helmets while riding tricycles and bicycles. Several suggestions for communicating helmet safety follow.

- Use information resources from the AAA Traffic Safety Department and the U.S. Consumer Product Safety Commission. Resources and contact information for both organizations are discussed in the following section.
- Many local health and public safety departments have traffic safety divisions. Resources available for promoting the use of helmets and bike safety may include public presentations designed for specific age groups, informational flyers for sending home to parents, or instructional material for children. These departments often have the responsibility to promote cycling safety in the community and

are prepared to bring their message of cycling safety to local schools and child care centers. Consider inviting a member of one of these departments to speak to the children you teach.

- Create a bulletin board that promotes the importance of wearing helmets when cycling. Select a highly visible location for the bulletin board so that both children and adults view its message. Feature pictures of children wearing helmets along with the cycling safety tips discussed earlier.
- Send home notes prior to beginning units on tricycle riding and roller skating asking parents to send in helmets. Include reminders in the notes for children to wear helmets at home while roller-skating or tricycle riding.
- Create the opportunity for all families to afford bike helmets by referring parents to local sources of low-cost helmets. If there is no local low-cost source of helmets, organize your own helmet purchase campaign. Local service organizations, such as Kiwanis, Rotary, or Elks, may be interested in joining you in the community project of providing low-cost helmets to families. Two highly recommended sources of low-cost bike helmets are Helmets R Us and CNS (Children-n-Safety) National Helmet Program. Refer to the "Resources" section at the end of this chapter for company addresses. Both companies sell helmets that meet the Consumer Product Safety Commission Bike Helmet Standards for approximately $5 each plus shipping and handling. Promotional packages organized by age groups and numbers of children are available. Consider contacting these companies, along with any others you may know, to obtain current pricing information and sales promotions, and then decide which company may best serve your helmet needs. Send home a promotional flyer complete with an order form and deadline. Encourage adults to spread the word. Refer to chapter 13 for further information about conducting a helmet campaign. Help make it possible for every child to wear a helmet!

CYCLING SAFETY CURRICULUM BOOKS AND KITS

Several high-quality curriculum kits are available to assist in the task of teaching cycling safety. The AAA Foundation for Traffic Safety is an outstanding, comprehensive source of materials for teaching cycling safety as well as bus safety, pedestrian safety, and school safety. Programs for young learners (three to seven years of age) are highlighted here. Resources are also available for older children. Share the AAA information with those who teach older children and let safety be an ongoing educational process. The following resources can be ordered for low cost from the AAA Foundation for Traffic Safety. Refer to the "Resources" section that follows for the AAA Foundation contact information.

- *The Teacher's Guide to Bicycle Safety: Kindergarten–Grade 8* is a free publication by the American Automobile Association Traffic Safety Department. The *Teacher's Guide* is designed "to help you meet student needs in the area of bicycle/traffic safety education. The suggested activities provide ways to implement bicycle safety into a daily classroom program through integration with language arts, math, science, and art curricula. Activities have been grouped by grade to take into account differences in student capabilities from kindergarten through eighth grade. Individual activities may also be modified to meet your own particular needs" (1988, 2).*
- The *AAA Traffic Safety Catalog* offers a wealth of resources for sale. Materials range from certificates and safety stickers to instructional videos, books, and pamphlets for distribution. Categories for catalog resources include the following:
    - **Bicycle safety and school bus safety** resources include storybooks for children in preschool through eighth grade, identification cards, posters, pamphlets, and a bicycle skill test for groups and rodeo events.
    - **School safety patrol** resources include safety patrol belts, badges, slickers, hats, a handbook, several pamphlets, certificates, badges, and a safety patrol test for children.
    - **Traffic safety education materials and poster program** resources include safety stories, activity books, posters, pamphlets, and teacher guides.
    - **Pedestrian safety, Halloween safety, preschool children, and the safest route to school** resources include separate pamphlets with safety tips for parents about each of these topics.
    - **School's open** resources include posters, pencils, litter bags, bumper stickers, rulers, and place mats with messages promoting safety.
    - **Occupant protection and alcohol countermeasures** resources include a variety of pamphlets and litter bags promoting safe transport of children.

*From American Automobile Association (AAA) Traffic Safety Department, 1988, *The teacher's guide to bicycle safety: Kindergarten—Grade 8* (Washington, DC: American Automobile Association).

- *Traffic Safety Materials: Millennium Edition Catalog* by the AAA Foundation for Traffic Safety includes videos and CD-ROMS on safety topics involving situations encountered by individuals from preschool through adulthood. Educational materials for young children include the following:
    - *Otto the Auto*, a comprehensive video series for children preschool through sixth grade covering bicycle safety, auto and pedestrian safety, pedestrian visibility, seat belt safety, and school bus safety. The four-video series is $40.
    - *Bicycle and Pedestrian Safety* videos teach older children how to ride a bike safely and share the road with motorists. The four-video series is $40.

RESOURCES

Sources for adapted tricycles and accessories:

Rifton Equipment
359 Gibson Hill Rd, Chester, NY, 10918-2321
Phone: 1-800-777-4244
Web site: www.rifton.com

FlagHouse Special Populations
601 FlagHouse Drive, Hasbrouck Heights, NJ 07604-3116
Phone: 1-800-793-7900
Web site: www.flaghouse.com

Source of Lemon Quat, a spray used to kill head lice:

Buckeye International
2700 Wagner Place, Maryland Heights, MO 63043-3471
Phone: 1-800-321-2583
Web site: www.buckeyeinternational.com

Companies selling inexpensive bike helmets:

Helmets R Us, Inc.
413 Oak Place, Suite 4/M, Port Orange, FL 32127
Phone: 1-800-438-3904
Fax: 1-386-788-7176
Web site: www.HelmetsRus.net

CNS (Children-n-Safety) National Helmet Program
1620 Industry Drive SW #C, Auburn, WA 98001
Phone: 1-253-333-2061
Phone: 1-800-642-3123
Fax: 1-800-414-5560
Web site: www.prorider.com

Source of bicycle safety materials:

AAA Foundation for Traffic Safety
607 14th Street NW, Suite 201, Washington, DC 20005
Phone: 1-202-638-5944
Phone: 1-800-993-7222
Fax: 1-202-638-5943
Web site: www.aaafoundation.org

Stories about riding bicycles for young children:

Brown, M. W. 1994. *Red light, green light.* New York: Scholastic.

Brown, M. 1996. *D.W. rides again.* Boston: Little, Brown and Co.

Shannon, D. 2002. *Duck on a bike*. New York: Blue Sky Press/Scholastic.

Wolff, A. 1999. *Stella and Roy*. Madison, WI: Turtleback Books.

chapter 11

Fitness and Nutrition

Helen reread the quote several times, reeling as she grasped the enormity of its implications. "[In 2001 there were] nearly twice as many overweight children and almost three times as many overweight adolescents as there were in 1980. Left unabated, overweight and obesity may soon cause as much preventable disease and death as cigarette smoking"* (U.S. Surgeon General 2001, Foreword). She looked at herself and the young children in her class and thought, "Yes, it is true. Just look at us. Several of us have become a bit heavy." Considering this a call to action, she decided that she *must* do something to help the overweight children in her charge achieve a healthier weight—but how?

THE FACTS ARE STARTLING and deeply disturbing. An epidemic of childhood obesity is occurring in the United States. Overweight and obesity are increasing in both genders and among all population groups. Most disturbing is the rate at which the percent of overweight and obese children is increasing. In 1999 an estimated 61 percent of U.S. adults were overweight or obese, and 13 percent of children and adolescents were overweight (U.S. Surgeon General 2001). At the current rate, one in four children will be overweight or obese soon. Already two out of three adults in the United States are overweight or obese! The major health problems likely to result from weight gain will exact a huge toll from each individual's quality of life and the nation's well-being as these children age.

Fortunately, something can be done to counter this trend. Most obese children were not born obese. They became obese over the years because of nutritional choices and activity patterns that favor obesity. Educators now have an opportunity and a responsibility to infuse their curricula with learning experiences that promote sound nutrition and an active

*Reprinted from the United States Surgeon General, 2001, *2001 Surgeon General's call to action to prevent and decrease overweight and obesity.* Available at www.surgeongeneral.gov/topics/obesity/calltoaction/toc.htm.

Children love learning about good nutrition. Health concepts can be reinforced in a playful way while in a tomato house.

lifestyle. Children can learn to eat better and be more active and in doing so pave the way to healthier, happier lives.

This chapter presents practical ideas to help you plan lessons and conduct activities to create an awareness, acceptance, and adoption of healthy eating and activity choices for young children. Learn how to use food picture cards, curriculum resources, and special events to educate young children about healthy food choices, the importance of exercise, and the basics of how our bodies work. The most powerful influence on children's fitness and nutritional habits will be what family adults and teachers model. View this chapter as a call to action if you, like many of us, are a little on the heavy side. We can use the pressing need to teach good nutrition and exercise habits to children as an opportunity to improve our own eating and exercise habits as well. We will serve as important role models and become healthier in the process.

OBESITY EPIDEMIC

Overeating or eating unhealthy foods, accompanied by a lack of sufficient exercise, ultimately leads to weight gain and, if unchecked, to obesity. Obesity brings with it an entourage of significant health problems including, but not limited to, diabetes and heart disease. These conditions can lead to premature death. The good news is that obesity can be prevented with good nutrition and regular physical activity.

The information that follows is from the foreword to the 2001 Surgeon General's Call to Action to Prevent and Decrease Overweight and Obesity, which you can read at www.surgeongeneral.gov/topics/obesity/calltoaction/toc.htm.

> Overweight and obesity may not be infectious diseases, but they have reached epidemic proportions in the United States. Overweight and obesity are increasing in both men and women and among all population groups. In 1999, an estimated 61 percent of U.S. adults were overweight or obese, and 13 percent of children and adolescents were overweight . . . . We are already seeing the tragic results from these trends. Approximately 300,000 deaths a year in this country are currently associated with overweight and obesity.*

Overweight children and adolescents are more likely to become overweight or obese adults; this concern is greatest among adolescents. Type 2 diabetes, high blood pressure, high blood lipids, and hypertension as well as early maturation and orthopedic problems also occur with increased frequency in overweight youth. A common consequence of childhood overweight is psychological—specifically discrimination. For the vast majority of individuals, overweight and obesity result from excess calorie consumption and/or inadequate physical activity (U.S. Surgeon General 2001). Thus, the promotion of a healthy diet and regular physical activity should be the cornerstone of any prevention or treatment effort.

EAT HEALTHY FOODS, BE MORE ACTIVE

The facts presented in the previous section clearly indicate where our young children are headed if current trends of overweight and obesity continue. The surgeon general's report recommends actions that are especially relevant for teachers and parents of young children. They are

*Reprinted from the United States Surgeon General, 2001, *2001 Surgeon General's call to action to prevent and decrease overweight and obesity.* Available at www.surgeongeneral.gov/topics/obesity/calltoaction/toc.htm.

Surgeon General's Call to Action to Prevent and Decrease Overweight and Obesity

- Ensure *daily, quality physical education* in *all* school grades.
- Reduce time spent watching television and in other similar sedentary behaviors.
- Build physical activity into regular routines and playtime for children and their families. Children should aim for *at least 60 minutes [of moderate physical activity on most days of the week].*
- Promote healthier food choices, including at least five servings of fruits and vegetables each day and reasonable portion sizes.
- Provide more food options that are low in fat, calories, and added sugars such as fruits, vegetables, whole grains, and low-fat or nonfat dairy foods.
- Reduce access to foods high in fat, calories, and added sugars and excessive portion sizes.

Reprinted from the United States Surgeon General, 2001, *2001 Surgeon General's call to action to prevent and decrease overweight and obesity.* Available at www.surgeongeneral.gov/topics/obesity/calltoaction/toc.htm.

listed on this page in "Surgeon General's Call to Action to Prevent and Decrease Overweight and Obesity."

All teachers and child care providers can play a vital role in educating children and families about the importance of healthy nutrition and regular physical activity. Fortunately, planning how to approach the topics of fitness and nutrition need not be overwhelming. In this chapter we share lesson plan ideas and describe movement activities that can help you start an effective fitness and nutrition education program.

LESSON PLANS FOR TEACHING FITNESS AND NUTRITION CONCEPTS

There are so many creative ways to teach young children basic fitness and nutrition concepts. You may want to do several lessons on fitness and nutrition during the month of February (Healthy Heart Month), as well as weave concepts about fitness and nutrition throughout the year's lessons. This section outlines some teacher-tested ideas that draw on the activities presented in part II of this book; activities in *Moving With a Purpose* (McCall and Craft 2000); and videos, games, and big books in the curriculum kits discussed later in this chapter. Big books (oversized books with simple text and large illustrations) are ideal for reading to an entire class because everyone can see the huge pages. They can be wonderful teaching tools in your fitness and nutrition lessons. We suggest the following lesson plan format:

1. Begin with a fitness warm-up.
2. Read the children a big book or have them view a short video introducing fitness and nutrition concepts.
3. Lead a physical activity to reinforce fitness and nutrition concepts.
4. Conclude with a cool-down and lesson summary.

The following four lesson plans illustrate fun and easy ways to help children learn basic fitness and nutrition concepts.

Lesson 1

Introduce the concepts of healthy foods and the heart as a muscle.

Warm-Up

Always start each movement lesson with a warm-up. This routine provides a structure that gives security to young children who feel more comfortable knowing what to expect. We suggest a vigorous warm-up to provide cardiovascular exercise and also to help the children get their wiggles out. Use upbeat music for fun, motivating warm-ups. Dictated music, which contains lyrics that instruct children in gross motor movements, is especially effective for warm-ups. Several CD selections of dictated music are suggested in chapter 3 on music. Here are a few of our favorites:

- "Get Ready, Get Set, Let's Dance" on the Greg and Steve's *Kids in Action* CD
- "Walking Down the Street" on Jeffrey Friedberg's *Bossy Frog* CD
- "Movin' Every Day" on the *Preschool Aerobic Fun* CD by Kimbo
- "On the Count of Five" (an old favorite) on the *Sally the Swinging Snake* CD by Hap Palmer

Nutrition Concepts

At the conclusion of the warm-up activity, ask the children to sit down and show them a short video on fitness and nutrition that presents the developmentally appropriate message: eat healthy food, be active, and avoid smoking to have a healthier heart. The video *HeartPower! Sing-Along* found in the *HeartPower! Level K–2* curriculum kit published by the American Heart Association (and further described on pages 169-170), is an excellent choice. Contact information for the American Heart Association is in the "Resources" section at the end of this chapter. For other videos that convey this healthy heart message, check with your local health department's nutrition extension, teacher center, library, or the American Heart Association.

After deciding that most of the children have accepted the video's messages that eating healthy food, being active, and avoiding smoking is important for a healthy heart, introduce the following physical activity to reinforce fitness and nutrition concepts.

Heartbeat

Cardiovascular endurance

How thrilling it is to see children's eyes light up as they hear their own hearts beat for the first time! Use this activity to teach children that the heart is a muscle that needs to be exercised to keep us healthy.

Overview

Use this simple running activity and a stethoscope to introduce children to the change in the sound of their hearts when they are sitting compared to when they have exercised vigorously.

Goals for Children

- Identify changes in their own heartbeat
- Develop cardiovascular endurance
- Learn to stop and go on cue

Equipment

- Stethoscope
- Cleaning alcohol and cotton
- Music and CD player

Equipment Tips

The following are three lively music selections:

- "Unlimited Megajam" on the *ESPN Presents: Jock Jams, Volume 4* CD
- "Sala Keba" by Papa Wemba on Putumayo's *One World* CD
- Volume one, track two on the Mayatek *Motion Series* CD

Refer to chapter 3 for additional music suggestions and information on ordering these CDs.

A stethoscope is included in the *HeartPower!* kit, which is referenced later in this chapter. Ask a school nurse or other medical personnel to borrow another. Others can be purchased separately if funds permit. If stethoscopes are unavailable, use toy stethoscopes or toilet paper rolls or paper towel rolls to listen to each other's hearts.

Preparation

Gather as many adults and stethoscopes as possible to help with this activity. One adult with a stethoscope for every four children minimizes waiting time.

Instructions

1. A good way to introduce this concept is to lead an activity in which children exercise vigorously and then are prompted to notice the changes in their heart rates. Begin by saying to the children, "Feel your chest over your heart. When we are sitting, our hearts are resting and beating slower. Now we are going to exercise, and our hearts will beat faster." Explain to older children that, "Our bodies have muscles to help us move. Muscles must be exercised to stay healthy. The heart beats faster because the muscles need more oxygen when exercising. The heart pumps the blood with the needed oxygen to the muscles, and the heart stays healthy because it is also exercising."
2. Instruct children to run in the same direction in a large circle for the duration of one song.
3. Turn on lively music. We suggest having children run continuously for three to four minutes, accompanied by energizing music, to increase their heart rates.
4. Then turn off the music and gather everyone together. Help children listen to their hearts beating through stethoscopes to give them a better understanding of what is happening to their hearts when they exercise. Give everyone an opportunity to listen to his or her own heart beating by positioning a stethoscope over the heart and putting the earplugs in the child's ears. Be sure to wipe the earplugs of stethoscopes with alcohol-soaked cotton between each use. When children smile or their eyes light up, you know that they have heard their own heart beating. A few children may be reluctant to allow you to place earplugs in their ears. Encourage them to put the stethoscope on their chest, reassuring them that nothing needs to go near their ears. Often these reluctant children will be willing to try the stethoscope's earplugs after seeing their peers use them.
5. Repeat the sequence of having the children run and then stop and listen to their hearts beating. Allow them to rest for a few minutes so their heart rates decrease before they listen to their hearts again. Then play the vigorous activity once more so they can again experience the difference in heart rate during rest and exercise. Help children first find their heartbeat with the aid of a stethoscope. Later they will be able to find it using only their hand placed

over their chest. Repeatedly call attention to the change in their heart rates as children move from sitting and listening to vigorous exercise.

Adaptations

Children who use any adapted mobility equipment can participate. Any form of exercise that will enable a child to elevate the heart rate is sufficient for this activity. For children who wear hearing aids, merely place the stethoscope earplugs over the hearing aids.

Variations

This simple activity needs no variations. Children at any level of ability should be able to identify their changing heart rate.

Changing the Space

- In a small space, ask children to jump in place. This will quickly elevate their heart rates.
- In a large space or outdoors, perform the activity as described.

Cool-Down and Lesson Summary

Cooling down is important to let the children's bodies gradually return to rest and relaxation. It also helps them calm themselves after the excitement of vigorous physical activity and prepares them to focus on classroom activities. The quickest way to alienate classroom teachers is to dismiss children from physical education while they are still in the heat of the vigorous activity and more likely to be loud and rowdy in the halls on their way back to the classroom. Take a few minutes at the end of the lesson to help children calm themselves while doing gentle stretches to peaceful music. Here are a few of our favorites from the list of calming music in chapter 3:

- "Für Elise" by Beethoven on the *Baby Beethoven* CD
- Track two on the *Tune Your Brain with Mozart* CD
- "Book of Days" on the Enya CDs *Shepherd Moons* or *Paint the Sky With Stars*

Refer to chapter 3 for additional suggestions and information on ordering these CDs. You may want to use one of a variety of relaxation sound machines that has a heartbeat as one of its soothing sounds.

Primary school children may enjoy two minutes of relaxation using guided imagery. Lead the relaxation in a calm, gentle voice. Instruct the children to imagine themselves in a warm, peaceful setting, relaxing each part of their body in turn. Walk among the children, leading the guided imagery and helping those who are having difficulty releasing muscle tension. As the children demonstrate that they are relaxed, quietly ask them in turn to get up, walk over to the door, and stand quietly in line for dismissal. Finding a transition that is comfortable for both you and the children is important for a successful conclusion to each movement lesson.

Lesson 2

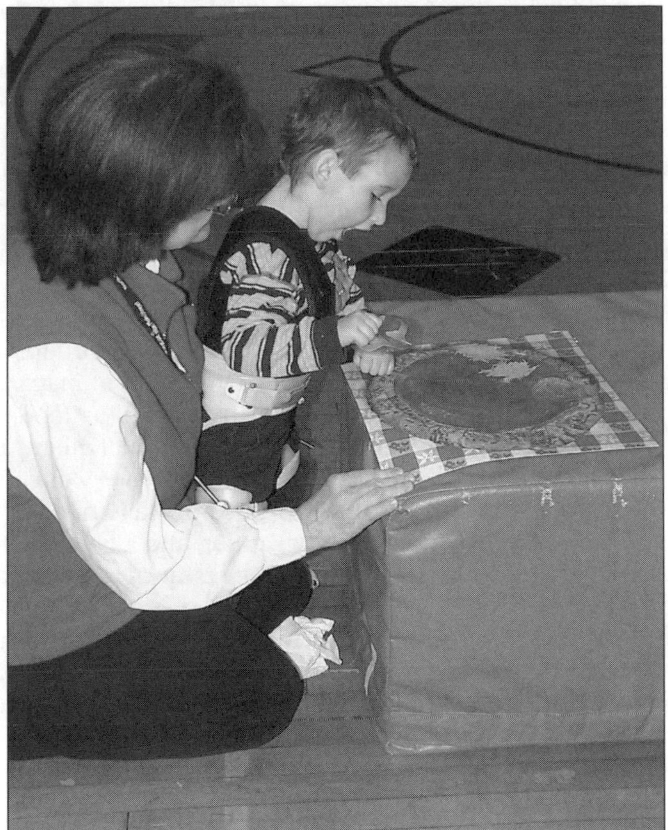

In this lesson children learn to identify healthy foods.

Warm-Up

Have the children warm up with a vigorous activity to dictated music. Refer to lesson 1 for further suggestions.

Nutrition Concepts

Introduce the concept of healthy and unhealthy foods and help children learn to identify them. In this second lesson, show the children a variety of foods they would be likely to eat, and have them identify and categorize them as healthy or unhealthy. Children may be able to name the foods, but may need assistance in categorizing them as healthy or unhealthy. Emphasize that healthy foods should be eaten often, but unhealthy foods should be eaten seldom and in small quantities, if at all. See the equipment sections for tips on how to display food items.

Either with pictures or actual foods, try to display the variety and ethnicity of healthy and unhealthy foods that children would be served at home or would encounter when eating out. Children will be interested in seeing fresh, healthy food from your own refrigerator and cupboard such as lettuce, potatoes, carrots, spinach, beans, brown rice, and so forth. You can make healthy and unhealthy food picture cards from magazine pictures. You can also use the large photos of food that come in the *HeartPower! Level K–2* curriculum kit, described later in this chapter.

Making Healthy and Unhealthy Food Picture Cards

Food picture cards, each with a photo of a single healthy or unhealthy food, are easy to make and serve as excellent props for fun activities about nutrition. These activities begin with conversations about nutritious food and end with a physical activity twist. Prepare for these fitness and nutrition activities by clipping pictures out of magazines that portray foods. Choose foods that are healthy as well as foods that are unhealthy and should be avoided or eaten only in small quantities. Have a ratio of at least four healthy food picture cards to every one unhealthy food picture card. Also collect food wrappers from fast food restaurants, including a french fry jacket, a burger wrapper, and a chicken strip box. Ask for unused wrappers and boxes from the restaurant. It's cheaper that way, and you won't need to eat the fast food.

Glue or tape the pictures and wrappers to 8 1/2-inch by 11-inch card stock that is cut in half to become 5 1/2 inches by 8 1/2 inches. Laminate or cover each picture card with contact paper so that it is durable enough to use year after year. Continue cutting and collecting until you have at least 50 food picture cards and wrappers that represent all levels of the food pyramid and both healthy and unhealthy foods. (Go to www.usda.gov/cnpp/KidsPyra/ for a food pyramid for two- to six-year-olds.)

Creating the cards is initially time consuming, but once you have them, the activity will require only a few moments of preparation time. Perhaps interested parents would be happy to volunteer to make the cards.

Identifying Healthy and Unhealthy Foods

Instruct children to sit together on a mat, carpet squares, or other designated gathering spot. Explain to the children that you will be holding up a picture of one kind of food. As they look at the picture, ask them to say the food's name, if they know it. It is fine to have several children giving the name at the same time. If the children are unable to identify the food, introduce it to them. If the children are more advanced, challenge them with more difficult questions such as, "Is this food a meat or vegetable?" or, "Where does this food belong in the food pyramid?" Expand the questions to teach other concepts. While holding a card with a picture of a banana, ask, "What color is the banana" and, "Does a banana grow on a tree or in the ground?" Present the cards in a mixed order so that a fast food follows an orange. Conclude by asking, "Is this a healthy food?" for each card.

As you hold up a picture of ice cream or a cookie or the french fry container, children will inevitably tell you how good these foods taste. This is a wonderful opportunity to have a discussion about quantity, size, and frequency. Be honest! You might say something like, "I like ice cream too, but should we eat ice cream for a snack after school and again before bedtime? Should we eat a giant bowl or a small bowl of ice cream? Should we eat one brownie occasionally as a treat or five brownies in one day?" Children love being part of these conversations, and the information just flows!

Salad Spinner

Cardiovascular endurance • Locomotor skills

This high-energy activity is a great way for children to practice distinguishing between healthy and unhealthy foods. This is also the perfect activity for when you have little prep time and no equipment.

Overview

This variation of Scrambled Eggs (McCall and Craft 2000, 116) has children exercising vigorously as they pretend to be various foods inside a salad spinner. Pretend that the room or outdoor playing area is a giant salad spinner and that all the children are the salad ingredients. Explain that when you call "salad spinner," the children move as directed—running, galloping, or jumping in a single direction around the open space. They are to continue moving until you call out the selected ingredient to add to the salad. This ingredient is the signal to stop and sit down. Continue adding new ingredients, alternately moving and stopping, until the salad is made. Then everyone pretends to eat the salad.

Goals for Children

- Develop locomotor skills
- Learn nutritional concepts

Equipment

No equipment is needed.

Equipment Tip

Children may not be familiar with a salad spinner, so the first time you play this activity you may want to show the children a salad spinner and demonstrate how it works.

Instructions

1. Ask the children to select the first ingredient to add to the salad spinner. This ingredient becomes the first signal to stop.
2. Ask a child to select a way for everyone to move such as run, walk backward, jump, or gallop. Begin the activity by explaining that when children hear you say "salad spinner," they are to jump around the room. When they hear you say "lettuce," they are to stop in place and sit down.
3. Continue playing the activity, adding new ingredients and using new movements for each round. Accept all of the children's suggestions of ingredients to add to the salad spinner, even the silly or unhealthy ones. You may have a salad containing carrots, cucumbers, french fries, and chocolate syrup.
4. When a child calls out a food, ask the group in a playful dramatic way, "Is this a healthy or unhealthy food?" Help the children identify foods that are good to eat regularly and those that should only be eaten occasionally, if at all.
5. Have children recall all of the ingredients already in the salad as they add each new ingredient. Begin with the most recent ingredient and go back to the initial ingredient. Practice in sequencing helps develop skills useful in retelling stories. Periodically review the rules about moving safely as the children continue to play the activity.
6. The activity ends when you decide that the salad has been spun. At that point you all pretend to eat it.

Adaptations

Children who have difficulty walking can use adapted equipment to aid their mobility. Consider pairing an adult with any child who may have a visual impairment to guide the child around the activity area.

Variations

Each time you play the activity, vary the healthy food dish you create. Pretend to make a fruit salad, a pasta salad, or a stir-fry. Two other fun and invigorating activities in this book are Roll Out the Bubble Wrap on page 39 and Suspended Noodle Jump on page 77. The cycling activities in chapter 10 provide cardiovascular exercise for children who have mastered the basics of pedaling. Most tag games also provide cardiovascular exercise. Any activity that has children moving the large muscles of their bodies continuously for several minutes, whether running, jumping, hopping, leaping, galloping, skipping, or dancing, provides a great cardiovascular workout.

Use whatever activity you favor. Just be sure that it provides plenty of large muscle movement to get children's hearts pounding through cardiovascular exercise.

Changing the Space

This activity works best in a large open space. In a small space, substitute another activity to provide a cardiovascular workout. Several options are listed in the "Variations" section.

Cool-Down and Lesson Summary

As the vigorous activity ends, once again gather the children together and ask them to put their hands on their chests to note how fast their hearts are beating. Conclude the lesson by asking questions such as the following to review key concepts about the heart:

- How big is your heart? (It is as big as my fist.)
- Where is your heart in your body? (It is in the middle of my chest.)
- What does your heart pump throughout your body? (My heart pumps blood.)

For older children, ask, "What does your blood do?" (Blood carries food and oxygen to all the cells of my body.)

Lesson 3

Identify healthy foods as well as review the location and function of the heart.

Warm-Up

Have the children warm up with a vigorous activity to dictated music. Refer to lesson 1 for further suggestions.

Nutrition Concepts

As the warm-up ends, gather the children together and read them a book about the heart to continue their fitness education. A good choice is the big book *Big News! Straight From the Heart* from the *HeartPower! Level K–2* curriculum kit referenced later in this chapter on pages 169-170. If this book is not available to you, select another children's book that teaches fitness and nutrition concepts from among those listed later in the chapter or from your local library. Point to the words as you read the book aloud so that children who are ready to read can begin to match words with their sounds.

Salad Run

Locomotor skills • Object, color, and shape recognition

This activity is a simple way to introduce young children to a variety of healthy foods and their names.

Overview

Salad Run is a variation of the Move and Match activities Pizza and Highway Patrol described in chapter 9. Children move between points A and B, gathering food theme cards to match the card that you display. As they gather the cards, they learn to recognize and name each food.

Goals for Children

- Identify a variety of healthy foods
- Develop locomotor skills

Equipment

- Food theme cards, with at least one card of each food per child, plus one identical card for demonstration. Playing with 10 children would require 11 identical strawberry cards, 11 carrot cards, 11 peas cards, 11 lettuce cards, 11 grape cards, and so forth.
- One large bin or plastic wading pool
- A colorful means of marking point A

Equipment Tips

Food theme cards showing pictures of healthy foods can be hand drawn or printed from clip art on a computer, cut out, then taped and laminated to index cards. Make several identical cards of each food.

Preparation

Scatter all the fruit and vegetable food theme cards on a mat or other safe surface at point B across the playing area. Place the large bin or plastic wading pool at point A, the starting point.

Instructions

1. Hold up a food theme card and ask children to find its match.
2. Children run across the area to point B. Here each child selects the food card that matches the card you are holding, returns with it to the starting point, and places the card in the large bin or pool. Change the challenge by instructing children to gallop, jump, or use roller skates when crossing to point B.
3. As you play these activities, call children's attention to the changes in their heart rate as they move from sitting and listening to vigorous activity. Also emphasize the importance of eating the healthy foods shown on the cards throughout the activity.
4. Continue until all the cards have been matched.

Adaptations

When teaching a child with a significant visual impairment, ask this child to move between points A and B, locating a ringing bell. As other children are learning to match pictures, this child is learning an important life skill of auditory tracking.

Variations

Other activity variations for introducing healthy food concepts include the following:

- Supermarket Sweep on page 111 and Thanksgiving Dinner on page 115 (a variation of Let's Make a Meal) in chapter 9 of this book
- Fruit Salad in chapter 7 of this book on page 82
- Stop and Go to Music and Tag–Vegetable Soup in *Moving With a Purpose* (McCall and Craft 2000, 120-121 and 136-137, respectively)

Changing the Space

- In small spaces, ask children to perform locomotor movements such as hopping, jumping, walking backward, or walking on tiptoes rather than running.
- In a large space or outdoors, play the activity as described.

Cool-Down and Lesson Summary

As the lesson ends, gather the children together to rest while you hold up the various food pictures used in the lesson. Ask the children to name each food, after which you may want to say, "Mmm,...it's good for you!"

Lesson 4

Identify healthy foods as well as introduce the location and function of the body's major organs.

Warm-Up

Have the children warm up with a vigorous activity. We suggest using one of the dictated music CDs listed in chapter 3.

Nutrition Concepts

After the warm-up, ask the children to sit with you and explain briefly that inside all humans are parts of our bodies we call organs. Together all of our organs must be healthy to keep us alive. The best way to keep our organs healthy is to eat healthy foods, exercise regularly, and get adequate rest. Continue the lesson by reading a book or showing a video that briefly explains the location and function of the bones, muscles, and major organs in our bodies. As you read the big book, point to each organ discussed. Assist children in finding the corresponding location of each organ on their own bodies.

We recommend the *Nose to Toes* big book from the curriculum kit by the same name, which is part of the *Primarily Health Series* described on pages 172-173 and listed in the "Resources" section at the end of this chapter. The kit also includes an organ apron. Teach the location and function of organs by wearing and referring to the apron. Detachable plastic replicas illustrating the size and location of several of the body's major organs are attached to the apron. The apron even comes with a hat designed to look like the brain. An alternative to purchasing the organ apron is making your own organs. Cut colored construction paper in the shape of the major body organs and laminate and adhere them with masking tape to your own clothes in their anatomically correct locations.

While identifying each organ, reinforce fitness and nutrition concepts such as the following:

- Our brain is located in our head. We protect our brain when we wear a helmet.
- Our lungs are located in our chest. We care for our lungs by not smoking.

- Our heart, located in the middle of our chest, is the strongest, most important muscle in our body. We exercise to keep it strong.
- Our stomach is in our belly. This is where the food goes when we eat healthy breakfasts, lunches, and dinners.
- Our intestines are also located in our belly. Food comes from the stomach and goes through the intestines where the nutrition is absorbed and what is not needed goes out of the body.

Even at the preschool level, children are ready to learn this information about their own bodies.

Mealtime

Locomotor skills • Object, color, and shape recognition

Here is an activity using realistic food images that will help children identify and make healthy food selections whether at the family dinner table or in a restaurant.

Overview

Children often need repeated practice to be able to identify healthy and unhealthy food. This activity enables them to see realistic images of food so they can envision how a healthy plate of food will look. Children move from point A to point B where they select pictures of healthy foods from among the healthy and unhealthy foods displayed, and return with them to point A.

Goals for Children

- Distinguish between healthy and unhealthy foods
- Develop locomotor skills

Equipment

- 50 healthy and unhealthy food picture cards (at least four healthy food picture cards per child)
- A table or stacked mats for displaying the food picture cards

Equipment Tips

Refer to lesson 2 on page 160 for instructions on making healthy and unhealthy food picture cards. Have a ratio of at least four healthy food picture cards for every one unhealthy food card.

You may want to use plastic foods instead of food picture cards. Constructive Playthings (www.cptoys.com) offers a variety of plastic foods at a reasonable price.

Preparation

Scatter the healthy and unhealthy food picture cards on the table or stacked mats at a point across the space from where the children begin.

Instructions

1. Begin the activity by briefly reviewing healthy and unhealthy foods. Show several of the healthy and unhealthy food picture cards to the children, flashing each card in turn and asking them whether it is a healthy or unhealthy food.
2. Explain that children are to move from the starting point A to point B. They are to select a healthy food picture card from among the healthy and unhealthy food picture cards displayed at point B and return with the card to point A.
3. Ask questions that require the children to identify foods as a review of the food concepts you just discussed. The type of question depends on the number of children involved. If you have a larger number of children, ask general questions such as, "Please bring me back a food card that is healthy and good for you." If you are working with a small group and have more cards per child, ask more specific questions such as the following:
   - Please bring me back a picture of a fruit.
   - Bring me back a picture of a healthy snack.
   - It is important to eat at least five servings of fruits and vegetables each day. Bring me back five fruit and vegetable cards.

Ask these questions enthusiastically to motivate the children.

Adaptations

Refer to earlier activities for adaptation suggestions.

Variations

If space allows, vary the locomotor challenge by asking the children to jump (or hop, gallop, or walk backward) down, find a picture of a healthy food for dinner, and jump back. Your young learners will love it.

Make a chart with two columns. Display the picture and name of each healthy food in one column and the picture and name of each unhealthy food in the other column. Encourage older children to use this chart for reference if they forget whether a food is healthy or unhealthy. The chart enables children to become more independent and resourceful in answering their own questions.

Changing the Space

This activity is easily played in a small or large space. Vary the locomotor movement requested to fit the available space.

Cool-Down and Lesson Summary

On the last day of the fitness and nutrition unit, again ask fitness and nutrition questions of the whole group as a "final exam." Then award a Fitness and Nutrition Certificate to each child. Use the certificates designed to be photocopied in the *Heart Power* kit or make your own. Include the major health message, a cartoon, and the name of the child. Send the certificates home with the children to stimulate discussion of healthy heart concepts with their families. A key to children adopting a healthy lifestyle is the establishment of healthy fitness and nutrition habits in their families.

FITNESS AND NUTRITION CURRICULUM BOOKS AND KITS

A wealth of health and fitness curriculum books and kits are available to help you get started. You might consider contacting your local health department to see if mini-grant funding is available for the purchase of curriculum kits. If you are a teacher, you might also ask your school's parent teacher organization for funds to purchase all or part of one or more kits. Another cost-reducing option is to purchasing individual learning tools from each kit. This strategy allows you to purchase a big book and other individual components at a significantly lower cost, which can be especially helpful when on a limited budget. You may then purchase additional kit components as funds become available.

The curriculum resources described in this section are the *HeartPower!* curriculum kit; the *Concept Health* big book series; and the two curriculum kits *Nose to Toes* and *Feeling Fit, That's It!,* which are part of the *Primarily Health Series* curriculum.

Heart Power

Two *HeartPower!* curriculum kits, one for pre-K and one for primary school children, are available from the American Heart Association (AHA). The kits are usually easiest to purchase through your local AHA office. Alternatively, refer to the "Resources" section at the end of the chapter for information on contacting the AHA National Center. The *Heart Power* curriculum kit is a great way to teach basic fitness and nutrition concepts to young children. Activity ideas using parts of the *Heart Power* curriculum kit are presented earlier in this chapter. Parent feedback from this curriculum is always positive! Many adults do not realize that young children are interested and eager to learn about healthy eating habits and maintaining cardiovascular fitness.

The Pre-K *HeartPower!* curriculum kit includes the following:

- A big book story titled *Big News! Straight From the Heart* accompanied by a narrative tape

- A large "HeartPower!" poster
- A large "Eat Healthy! Play Healthy! Live Healthy!" poster depicting healthy food and ways young children can be physically active
- A large "Take a Look Inside of You" poster
- A stethoscope
- Sing-along music and lyrics
- A teacher's resource guide
- Activity cards that include movement activities to promote cardiovascular fitness. The activities involve many locomotor movements including running, jumping, galloping, and skipping.

The primary school *HeartPower!* curriculum kit contains similar materials with the addition of eight copies of the book *Be Like the Animals* for children to read.

Contact your local county American Heart Association to learn how to obtain the *HeartPower!* curriculum kit. The kit is expensive to purchase outright, retailing for almost $300, yet it may be provided for a nominal charge to organizations that assist with AHA fund-raising efforts. It has been our experience that teachers who demonstrate a commitment to using the kit to enhance the nutrition and fitness education of children are often able to receive it from the AHA for minimal cost or for no cost at all.

The *HeartPower!* Web site (www.americanheart.org/presenter.jhtml?identifier=3003357) has several free lesson ideas and activities that teachers can download and print directly from the Web site. You can print the entire *Big News! Straight From the Heart* story as a low-cost alternative to purchasing it in the big book format.

Concept Health

Concept Health offers a big book series on health that is authored by Anne G. Jones. Each book sells for around $7. Their story lines capture children's attention from start to finish. These books have recently gone out of print, but are still available at early education convention trade shows and some local educational supply stores. Big book titles on health topics suitable for young children include the following:

- *How the Body Works*
- *Your Brain and Your Senses*
- *Your Eyes*
- *Your Ears*
- *Your Skin*
- *Your Bones and Muscles*
- *Digestion and Energy*
- *Your Heart*
- *Your Lungs*
- *Your Teeth*
- *Growing and Changing*
- *Staying Healthy and Fit*

- *Eating Healthy Foods*
- *Exercise and Rest*
- *Drugs, Alcohol, and Smoking*
- *Safety at Home*
- *Safety Outside Your Home*
- *Your Health and Your World*
- *Air, Water, and Your Health*
- *When People Get Sick*
- *Physically Challenged People*
- *Feeling Good About Yourself*
- *People Who Help You Stay Healthy*

Big book stories are stimulating educational tools that are easy to use outdoors or in a classroom, gymnasium, or home. They are fun to read aloud because all the children can easily view the large pages. Simply gather children together and use the information in a big book as an introduction to physical activity time, snack time, or story time.

Use conventional-size children's books about fitness and nutrition as an alternative if you do not have access to these big books. The Constructive Playthings catalog (www.cptoys.com) offers titles on body awareness and nutrition.

Primarily Health Series

The *Primarily Health Series* is a comprehensive, effective, but expensive curriculum for teaching an integrated health curriculum to children in preschool through grade three. The series comprises 12 big books, each with a corresponding teacher's guide and resource kit. Each kit helps children learn about a specific health topic. Activities in the kits also incorporate skills in language arts and other areas of the curriculum (Comprehensive Health Education Foundation 1995). Each health topic is introduced with a focus lesson and a reading of a big book. This popular program was created by the Comprehensive Health Education Foundation (CHEF) with the input of children, nurses, educators, and national health and education experts.

Each of the 12 *Primarily Health Series* kits costs approximately $300. The Wright Group is ending distribution of these excellent kits. They have a limited number of kits in stock and will make them available to those organizations who already have accounts with the Wright Group. If you are unable to obtain the kits through them, contact CHEF to determine whether another distributor has been located. These excellent resource kits are worth the extra effort needed to obtain them. Refer to the "Resources" list at the end of this chapter to order the *Primarily Health Series* from the Wright Group.

The *Primarily Health Series* uses simple language to teach children about health topics (Comprehensive Health Education Foundation 1995). The activities in each of the 12 kits are presented in a variety of ways to appeal to children with different learning styles. Health concepts are presented in big-book and pupil-book formats as well as through hands-on activities. The teacher guide gives suggestions for using the kits in integrated units (Comprehensive Health Education Foundation 1995).

The title (and focus) of each curriculum kit in this 12-part series is as follows:

- *Feeling Fit, That's It!* (fitness and nutrition)
- *Friends All Around* (disabilities)
- *Good Grief! Good Grief!* (healthy habits)
- *How Do You Feel?* (feelings)
- *It's Up to Me* (making choices)
- *Nose to Toes* (the human body)
- *Our Friend* (the environment)
- *We Are Family* (family changes)
- *What's Next?* (emergencies and safety)
- *When I'm Sick* (disease prevention)

- *Where's Mitten?* (loss and change)
- *Play It Safe* (outdoor safety)

According to the teacher's guide (Comprehensive Health Education Foundation 1995, 4), each kit is intended "to meet objectives across the curriculum such that children learn health concepts while also learning to enjoy music, express an idea creatively, participate in physical activity, and acquire skill participating in group activities."

An attractive feature of each curriculum kit is that the content can be adapted for children in preschool through third grade. Each kit has a teacher's guide of over 100 pages filled with seemingly endless ideas for teaching using the curriculum kit. Children love the physical activities and musical rhythms and songs that address each topic. The game boards, activity cards, and other materials are durable enough to withstand years of children's use. You may want to share the kits with instructors in other grade levels and disciplines to create a truly integrated approach to teaching. Each of these 12 kits offers a wealth of resources for teaching specific topics. The kits *Feeling Fit, That's It!,* and *Nose to Toes* are described in the following sections.

Feeling Fit, That's It!

The *Feeling Fit, That's It!* curriculum focuses on the topics of fitness and nutrition. As with all the CHEF kits, the information is rich in content and developmentally appropriate for young children. Health objectives include recognizing why we need to make healthy choices, choosing healthy snacks, identifying foods on the Food Guide Pyramid, and explaining how exercise affects the body (Comprehensive Health Education Foundation 1995).

From making a broccoli headband to creating a healthy pizza with paper cutouts from the resource guide, the activities in the curriculum guide are age appropriate and easily adapted to your particular needs. Children enjoy using the excellent hands-on learning materials such as the static sticker pizza toppings used in playing Put-Together Pizza and the sheets of healthy foods used in playing with the food pyramid. We find that a quick wipe with a damp cloth enables these static stickers to be used again and again. Use the kit's resources to play the activities described in the teacher's guide; use the kit's stickers and cards to create your own Move and Match activities, as described in chapter 9; or use the kit's food pictures in the food card activities described earlier in this chapter. The resources in this kit are fantastic, however you choose to use them!

Nose to Toes

This curriculum kit teaches children about the human body. "*Nose to Toes* gives young children an exciting introduction to their bodies—from the outside in! Children learn about their skin, muscles, bones, joints and several major internal organs with exposure to visually stimulating, hands on learning experiences" (Comprehensive Health Education Foundation 1995, 4). The complete curriculum kit sells for over $300, so you may want to initially purchase only the kit's big book and the organ apron. Wearing the organ apron, described earlier in this chapter in the section "Lesson Plans for Teaching Fitness and Nutrition Concepts," helps captures children's attention. They are intrigued and listen intently as you prepare to read a book wearing an apron covered with human organs!

Use the information in this chapter and other information that you may have to help the children in your care learn about the importance of good nutrition and daily exercise. Then help them develop these healthy habits. The benefits can last a lifetime.

RESOURCES

Following are some organizations to contact for information on nutrition and fitness:

American Heart Association
National Center
7272 Greenville Avenue
Dallas, TX 75231
Phone: 1-800-AHA-USA-1 or 1-800-242-8721
Web site: www.americanheart.org

Wright Group
220 East Danieldale Road
Desoto, TX 75115
Phone: 1-800-648-2970
Fax: 1-800-593-4418
Web site: www.WrightGroup.com

Following are some resources that you can use to teach fitness and nutrition in your classroom:

Brown, M. 1995. *D.W. the picky eater.* Boston: Little, Brown and Co.

Child, L. 2000. *I will never not eat a tomato.* Cambridge, MA: Candlewick Press.

Hoberman, M.A. 2001. *The seven silly eaters.* San Diego, CA: Harcourt Children's Books.

Jones, A.G. 1992. *Concept Health Series.* Cleveland, OH: Modern Curriculum Press.

Leedy, L. 1996. *The edible pyramid: Good eating every day.* Lebanon, IL: Pearson K-12.

Sharmat, M. 1989. *The terrible eater.* New York: Scholastic.

The following events and resources are geared specifically to promote healthy lifestyle habits. Go to the following Web sites to get the information necessary to participate.

International Walk to School Day

www.walktoschool-usa.org and www.iwalktoschool.org

These Web sites have great ideas and resources for successful events on Walk to School Day.

Creative Walking, Inc.

www.creativewalking.com

This site offers a number of low-cost walking programs and resources for teachers and children interested in starting a school- or community-wide walking program.

National TV-Turnoff Week

http://tvturnoff.org

Join millions of children and adults in TV-Turnoff Week, which takes place each April. A contract is sent home in which family adults and children agree to a specific number of days or time within a day that the adults and children will not watch TV. At the week's end the contract is signed and returned to school. A certificate is awarded to those children participating. Refer to chapter 13 under the month of April for more information about this event.

Eat Smart, Play Hard

www.fns.usda.gov/eatsmartplayhard

This Web site offers schools, health workers, and educators ideas for promoting good nutrition and regular physical activity. It is part of the USDA Eat Smart, Play Hard campaign. It includes numerous materials that can be downloaded and customized.

All Children Exercising Simultaneously (ACES)

members.aol.com/acesday

Participation in ACES is an excellent way to bring attention to the importance of regular physical activity. Refer to chapter 13 under the month of May for ideas about how you can promote regular exercise as part of this international event.

chapter 12

Lucy the Whale

Linda was strolling through the convention exhibit hall when she saw a black dome arching above the top of the curtain walls in the next aisle. Curious, she approached the booth and saw many people in line. She heard the hum of an electric fan. Rounding the corner, Linda stopped in amazement and stared, mouth open, at an enormous inflated whale stretched out before her. What would this be for? she wondered. Linda quickly joined the line and after a few minutes eagerly entered Lucy the whale. While inside Lucy, Linda had many ideas for using Lucy as a motivator in her movement program. Directly after touring this 55-foot (20 m) inflated sea mammoth, Linda began her inquiries about how she could get her own whale to use with her young students. When she learned she could easily build her own whale that would last for many years at a total cost of less than $100, Linda beamed as she imagined the wide-eyed excitement and exuberance of the youngsters in her program when they experienced Lucy the whale.

CHILDREN LOVE LUCY THE WHALE. They are in awe of her size and thrilled to step inside her 55-foot-long (20 m) body to learn and play. After you have built this highly durable inflatable whale, she will be the buzz of your school or center, providing many opportunities for fun-filled learning and good publicity for your program. Lucy offers so much for surprisingly little money and can be used by many different groups throughout each year and over many years. Lucy is an inexpensive modification to your teaching environment that is relatively easy to make, use, and store, and she is guaranteed to be a huge success. Build Lucy and see for yourself!

In this chapter we discuss reasons for including Lucy the Whale in your movement curriculum and give you creative movement lesson plan ideas for activities with Lucy. We also explain how to purchase the instructions for building Lucy from her creators at Wheelock College, discuss sources of funding to cover the cost of materials, and explore ways to use Lucy to gain positive publicity for your program.

WHO IS LUCY THE WHALE?

Lucy is a life-size, homemade, plastic skinned, inflatable model of a real whale that measures 55 feet (20 m) in length and 8 feet (3 m) in diameter. In the two minutes it takes to inflate her with a box fan, Lucy becomes an impressive and compelling area for movement activities and interdisciplinary learning experiences that are guaranteed to motivate and captivate young learners of all ages. The required construction materials, including sheets of plastic material and packing tape, can be purchased at a local hardware store. Lucy deflates quickly and is surprisingly easy to set up, carry, and store.

Here are several excellent reasons for including Lucy the Whale in your curriculum:

- Lucy is guaranteed to be a huge success with children, staff, and parents. She is a whale of a motivator for children, she makes teaching fun, and parents love to hear their children talk excitedly about playing inside a whale!

Figure 12.1 Lucy the whale adds great motivation to any movement program.

- Lucy provides a novel area for children to experience movement activities, increasing their attention and reducing behavior problems that usually follow boredom.
- Lucy is easily unrolled in three minutes and inflated in an additional two minutes. One person can do the job alone.
- Lucy is easy to transport and store. Once deflated, Lucy can be rolled tightly and placed in a large duffel bag, a 35-gallon plastic bin, or a garbage can. For even easier transport and storage, use a container on wheels.
- Lucy is affordable to construct and easy to maintain. She is durable enough to withstand the play of preschool and elementary children. Rips in her side are easily repaired with clear tape.

Constructing Lucy is surprisingly easy. Read on for information about where to order instructions from which you can construct Lucy in five hours, getting local help in building Lucy, and using Lucy to garner positive publicity for your program.

Ordering Instructions for Building Lucy

Purchase the clear and easy-to-follow instructions for making Lucy through WhaleNet at Wheelock College, 200 The Riverway, Boston, MA 02215. WhaleNet is an interactive information resource on the World Wide Web sponsored by Wheelock College with funding from the National Science Foundation. Lucy is one of several interdisciplinary curriculum resources found on the WhaleNet Web site. Write WhaleNet at Wheelock College or log onto WhaleNet (http://whale.wheelock.edu/whalenet-stuff/LucyPage.html) for information on how to order the instructions for building Lucy the whale, or contact the principal investigator and creator, listed in the "Resources" section at the end of this chapter. The cost of the instructions is less than $15. The site offers extensive information on whales and marine mammals of the North Atlantic Ocean. Integrated curriculum ideas on WhaleNet are geared to young learners as well as older students. Elementary science lessons to accompany the whale project are included; these lessons can be adapted for young learners.

Generating Interest in Building Lucy

Lucy offers the opportunity for interdisciplinary learning and a cooperative building experience. For elementary teachers, Lucy can be the catalyst for working with science, math, or social studies teachers within the elementary school or with secondary classes across the district. One example might involve asking a high school science or math teacher to take on the construction of Lucy as a class project to enliven the study of marine life in science or fractions and ratios in math. Those who build Lucy might be invited back to enjoy seeing, and perhaps to work with, younger children excitedly playing and learning inside Lucy. After you have laid the groundwork by creating school, district, or community interest in building Lucy, you must fund the project, acquire the materials, have Lucy built, publicize the project, and most important, use Lucy to teach children.

Funding Lucy

Funds to purchase materials for the construction of Lucy can come from any one of several resources.

- If your school has a parent teacher organization (PTO), approach the organization with a proposal listing the purpose of the project, curricular goals, and expected costs. Feature photos from the WhaleNet Web site so they can better understand the project. Ask if the organization would be willing to fund the project.
- Conduct a bottle drive, bake sale, or penny drive to fund Lucy. Ask the children for their family's permission to bring in spare coins from home.
- Conduct a community fund-raiser. Collect money in a jar, box, or envelope decorated with pictures of the whale and an explanation of the project. Donors are more willing to contribute when they can see what their money will build.
- Present your proposal to a local business or civic organization. Ask if they would be willing to support this very unique project.

Gathering Lucy's Materials

The materials needed to construct Lucy are minimal. In fact, you might have the feeling that you are short of supplies when you finish buying what you actually need! The plans call for

- enough clear or black rolls of plastic to accommodate the size Lucy will become,
- clear packing tape,
- scissors,
- string,
- a black marker, and
- a tape measure.

All materials are readily available at your local hardware store. You have the option of buying just rolls of clear plastic or a combination of rolls of black and clear plastic. One option yields an all-clear whale, and the other option yields a half-black and half-clear whale. We recommend making a half-black and half-clear whale. Young children are generally less tentative about stepping inside a huge whale when they can see out through one clear plastic side, and of course the black side makes Lucy look like a real whale!

Constructing Lucy

Lucy requires approximately five hours of construction time. Remember that once you have constructed Lucy, you will need less than five minutes to unroll and inflate her each time you use her. There are many ways an enterprising adult might recruit help with this construction project. Consider the following ideas, and remember to capture and share the excitement of constructing Lucy on videotape!

- Ask parents or scout troops to help construct Lucy over a weekend.
- Ask middle or high school students to volunteer on the construction for one hour daily over five school days as a science or mathematics project.
- Lucy's construction might also become a project for combined classes of an entire school or camp population, with adult supervision. Elementary age children, with adult guidance, are capable of assisting with cutting and taping. Preschool children may be too young to actually construct the whale, but they can still enjoy the opportunity to observe and ask questions as the project unfolds. They will be very happy to be invited to place a piece of tape on a plastic seam.

Determine a place for the construction. Because Lucy is 55 feet (20 m) long when complete, a school cafeteria or gymnasium might be ideal. A large lawn or playing field may work well too in fine weather. If the dimensions of Lucy are too big for your space, scale back the plans to make a smaller whale. Consider constructing a 35-foot (12 m) whale. If time and space allow, construct both and give children the choice of going in the big whale or the little whale. Add to the fun by organizing a contest to name the smaller whale.

Publicizing Lucy and Thanking Sponsors

After receiving the funds and constructing Lucy, be sure to recognize those who have donated money and time. Consider placing a big thank-you on a bulletin board that is visible to everyone entering the building. Also, write letters of thanks for submission in local newspapers as well as directly to the sponsors. Refer to chapter 13 under the month of March for ways to bring positive attention to your program by publicizing Lucy the Whale.

INTEGRATING LUCY INTO YOUR CURRICULUM

Lucy provides fantastic motivation for movement activities. Take some of the movement activities normally conducted in an open space and conduct them in Lucy. Activities become new and exciting again when played inside a whale! The first time you introduce Lucy, begin with her deflated. The children will be so excited as the fan is turned on and Lucy begins to inflate. Remember to review the following important safety rules for behavior inside Lucy before allowing the children to go in.

Important Safety Precautions for Lucy

When using Lucy with young children, a few precautions will make the experience safer and more enjoyable.

Allow children to choose whether to go inside Lucy. Initially there may be a few reluctant children who prefer to remain outside watching and listening to those already inside before joining their classmates inside this huge whale.

Establish boundaries inside the whale. Preschool children do not usually understand that running up the side of the whale makes it tip over. And if they do understand this, they may be tempted to try it. Help them avoid this temptation by placing clearly designated boundaries inside Lucy once she is inflated. Lay mats or a large carpet runner down the inside of Lucy to show where children can move. This allows adults to use positively worded instructions such as, "Stay on the mat, please," and avoids ambiguous, negative instructions such as, "Don't go so far to the side." Position the runner so that it ends several feet short of the box fan in the whale's tail.

Further reinforce that children are not to go to either end of the whale by placing stop signs a few feet from the whale's nose and tail. Make the octagon stop sign from red paper and laminate it for durability. Tape the sign to a plastic tube or pole and slide the pole through the top of a construction cone to hold the sign upright. Remind the children what the stop sign means. These precautions can be very successful when coupled with adult supervision.

Movement Activities With Lucy

Lucy the Whale provides an ideal opportunity to integrate the theme of whales and other ocean mammals into lessons in movement. Young children will be extremely motivated to learn when they see Lucy. Several activities are listed in the WhaleNet packet for elementary age children. Activity station ideas developed by Renée McCall are listed here.

Set up one station inside Lucy and one or more other stations throughout the remaining open activity area. Plan a combination of stations so that only one requires close adult supervision and the others can be conducted safely with general supervision. Setting up these stations the first time will require a bit of preparation, but if you label and store the equipment carefully, subsequent setups will go much more quickly. We recommend repeating these activities two or three times, creating a unit involving Lucy the Whale. This repetition allows children the opportunity to fully experience each of the stations. Change the combination of stations as you wish. Mix station suggestions listed under A Day on the Ocean with those under A Day at the Beach. Add your own ideas for stations to create combinations that work well in your setting.

Lucy provides an ideal centerpiece for an integrated curriculum. Classroom teachers may want to read stories about whales and marine life on the days you conduct the Lucy activities. Delightful stories about whales that are ideal for reading to young children are listed in the "Resources" section at the end of this chapter. Music teachers may want to teach songs about life on the ocean, fishing, or going to the beach. Plan lessons with other teachers in your program so children are singing, reading, drawing, and playing activities with a marine theme throughout the day. Begin each lesson with a warm-up, varying the music that you select.

A Day on the Ocean

Locomotor skills • Motor planning
Muscular strength and endurance • Object control

Children have so much fun pretending to spend the day out on the ocean, fishing off the boat, swimming in the ocean waves, and moving in the belly of a whale. Because they adore Lucy, they are motivated to do just about any movement activity that includes her.

Overview

Create four movement stations that relate to the ocean theme—three stations in the area surrounding Lucy and the fourth station inside Lucy.

- Station 1: Hoist a rope while pretending to haul in a fish.
- Station 2: Climb up and roll down while pretending to swim in ocean waves. Toss and catch beach balls.
- Station 3: Jump and clap to trigger a motion-sensitive toy fish to sing.
- Station 4: Twist and bend while pretending to swim in the belly of a whale.

Add your own station ideas or modify any activity as needed to make a fun Day on the Ocean.

Goals for Children

- Develop upper body strength
- Practice motor planning
- Learn to throw and catch
- Learn to jump

Equipment

- Beach Boys music, or other beach music, and a CD player
- Station 1—Go Fish: Fishing poles made from the equipment described in the activity Go Fish in chapter 5
- Station 2—Swim in the Waves: Tires covered with mats, beach balls
- Station 3—Billy the Big Mouth Bass: Motion-sensitive toy fish that sings
- Station 4—In the Belly of a Whale: Lucy the whale with mats or carpet runners and stop signs inside her for safety

Equipment Tips

If mats are not available for the station Swim in the Waves, simply stack tires to create a low mound. Then change the activity to pretend to climb over rocks along the shoreline. Be sure to clean the tires and check that no steel belts are exposed.

Billy the Big Mouth Bass is a novelty toy. Check at garage sales and ask around to determine whether anyone is willing to donate one that has lost its novelty in their home.

Preparation

Create stations that relate to the ocean before the lesson. Set up the In the Belly of a Whale station inside Lucy. Set up other stations throughout the remaining open activity area. Remember to plan a combination of stations so that only one requires close adult supervision and the others can be conducted safely with general supervision.

Instructions

Briefly explain the stations, keeping these comments to a maximum of three minutes to prevent restlessness among young children. Invite the children to go to whichever station they wish and to change stations whenever they wish. Giving children the freedom to choose what they want to do and when they want to change will eliminate a host of behavior difficulties. Play the Beach Boys music to signal that children may begin playing at the stations. At the end of the lesson, stop the music to signal that the children are to stop what they are doing and listen for instructions.

- Station 1—Go Fish: Make a station where children pretend to be fishing. Refer to the activity Go Fish on page 58 in chapter 5. Attach inflatable pool toys, especially those in the shape of fish and whales, or tie plastic fish onto the cones that the children haul up. Add paper fish in the plastic wading pool where the children release their fish.

- Station 2—Swim in the Waves: Create pretend waves on which children can roll, crawl, and slither. Pile tires high and low, following the instructions for Mountains and Valleys described in McCall and Craft (2000, 81-82). Lay wrestling mats over the top of the piled tires to create the effect of undulating ocean waves. Encourage the children to play in the waves, crawling up one side and rolling down the other. This activity is ideal for including children who are nonambulatory who can crawl, roll, scoot, and slide along with the other children. Add beach balls for children to toss and catch as they move.
- Station 3—Billy the Big Mouth Bass: Buy or borrow a motion-sensitive toy such as Billy the Big Mouth Bass that mounts on the wall. Billy turns and sings when it detects motion. Place Billy high enough on a shelf or wall so children need to jump or reach up for their motion to be detected. Prompt children to jump up and clap to get Billy to sing.
- Station 4—In the Belly of a Whale: Encourage the children to move freely within the boundaries inside the whale, swimming on their tummies, crawling, or rolling around in Lucy's belly. Children may also want to simply run or gallop through the whale. This can be done safely if all of the children first sit at one end of the whale and a few children take turns running or galloping. To keep the waiting time brief, this activity is best done with small groups of children. Help young children learn the names of the various locomotor movements as they perform each one.

Adaptations

Provide at least one station that accommodates each child with special needs. Children who are nonambulatory can be successful at the Swim in the Waves and Go Fish stations. Go Fish and In the Belly of a Whale are both ideal for children with limited sight or mobility. Position Billy the Big Mouth Bass at a height that will prompt children with limited range of motion to extend their upper limbs as high as possible to trigger his singing.

Variation

Vary the activity at the station inside Lucy. Substitute 52 Pickup, which is described in chapter 4. Ask the children to pick up small plastic or paper fish instead of plastic spoons. Challenge each child to find all the fish that match the example you display.

Changing the Space

Activities involving Lucy are suitable for a large indoor space with a clean, smooth floor. We caution you about inflating her outdoors. Be sure that there is safe access to an electrical outlet for the fan. Be aware that any stray stones and sticks may quickly puncture her sides, requiring repairs with clear packing tape.

A Day at the Beach

Locomotor skills • Motor planning • Object control

Is summer months away? Then now is the perfect time to bring out Lucy the Whale and pretend to spend a day at the beach. Dress for the sun, play summertime music, and frolic by the shore. This activity is a wonderful way to motivate children to practice movement skills while engaging in dramatic play.

Overview

Create four stations that relate to spending a day at the beach—three outside Lucy and one inside Lucy.

- Station 1: Toss and catch a ball while pretending to play beach volleyball.
- Station 2: Jump off a low object while pretending to jump off a dock into the water.
- Station 3: Practice maneuvering a fishing line over a fish while pretending to fish from a pier.
- Station 4: Negotiate an obstacle course while pretending to move through the inside of a whale.

Add your own station ideas to make a fun Day at the Beach.

Goals for Children

- Improve throwing and catching
- Learn to jump off an object
- Develop eye–hand coordination
- Develop motor planning

Equipment

- Beach Boys music and CD player
- Station 1—Beach Ball Volleyball: Rope and eyebolts, cloth for draping over the stretched rope, several beach balls
- Station 2—Jump Off the Dock: A low object from which to jump, mats or several pillows to create a soft landing area
- Station 3—Fishing With Poles: A rocking boat, common in preschools, for the children to fish from; plastic toy fishing poles and fish; blue mats; carpeting or some other way to designate the boundary of the fishing area
- Station 4—Mini-Obstacle Course Inside Lucy: Tunnels or pool noodle hurdles

Equipment Tips

Fishing With Poles: If a rocking boat is not available, use a large box with low sides so the children can simulate stepping into and sitting in a boat. Be sure that the children remain seated when using fishing poles.

Young children often lack the coordination to successfully catch fish using the commercially available toy fishing poles and fish. An easier alternative is to tape a Velcro strip (the loop side) onto the hook. Then tape the corresponding Velcro strip (the hook side) onto each of several fish theme cards. Children appear to catch fish when the two sides of the Velcro meet and adhere to each other.

Alternatively, make your own fishing poles using two-foot wooden dowels and two-foot lengths of string. Make a notch with scissors near the end of the dowel to hold the tied string in place. Attach a magnet instead of a hook at the end of the fishing line. Finally, attach a paper clip to each of several fish theme cards. The magnet will attach to the paper clip so that the children appear to have caught a fish.

Preparation

- Create stations that relate to the beach. Set up the mini-obstacle station inside Lucy. Set up other stations outside her throughout the remaining open activity area. Plan the combination of stations so that only one requires close adult supervision.
- Post a sign reading “Beach Days” and play some Beach Boys music in the background.
- To underscore the beach theme, wear summer clothing yourself and bring beach towels for children to lie on while doing the cool-down at the end of the lesson.

Instructions

Briefly explain each station, and then invite the children to go to any station they wish when the music starts. Children appreciate the freedom to choose to change stations whenever they wish.

- Station 1—Beach Ball Volleyball: Play Beach Ball Volleyball using the volleyball lead-up idea described on page 68 in chapter 5. Adjust the net height so that it is somewhere between head and waist height on the children. Simply let the children toss or hit beach balls over the net. Do not expect young children to share only one ball, hit a ball only once in a row, or hit the ball no more than three times before it goes over the net. Instead, provide plenty of balls and let the children simply volley, bat, or catch, and then throw the balls back and forth over the net.
- Station 2—Jump Off the Dock: Create a station in which children practice the skill of jumping off an object. Pile pillows on a crash mat and have the children jump off a low object into the pillows. Children can pretend they are

jumping off a dock into the water and swimming away. For safety, stress that no diving is allowed.

- Station 3—Fishing With Poles: Scatter fish around the designated fishing area. Explain that children are to sit in the boat when they enter the fishing area. From this seated position they can fish using any of the poles and fish described earlier. This station can accommodate two to four children at a time, depending on the size of the fishing box or boat. Remind the children to leave the poles in the fishing boat when they leave the station.
- Station 4—Mini-Obstacle Course Inside Lucy: Create a mini-obstacle course in the whale in which children crawl through a few plastic or fabric tunnels and over two or three hurdles to get from Lucy's nose to her tail. Refer to chapter 6 for ideas about using foam noodles. Avoid any climbing that would allow children to reach the top of the whale.

Adaptations

Be sure to provide at least one station that accommodates each child with special needs.

- In Beach Ball Volleyball, place any children who have limited strength or mobility directly in front of the net so they can merely drop the ball over the net to the other side. Put bells inside beach balls to add auditory cues for children with limited vision.
- In Jump Off the Dock, physically assist any children who are unable to jump independently. This enables all children to experience the sensation of their bodies in the air. Stress that the children should always jump feet first for safety.
- In Fishing With Poles, an adult may help facilitate positioning the pole over the fish.
- Modify the mini-obstacle course so that it remains challenging for children at varying skill levels.

Variations

Adapt the Move and Match activities described in chapter 9 so the children can play them inside the whale. Children will love this! Consider changing the game Pizza on page 108 in chapter 9 to become Fishes instead. Create theme cards of whales and fish. Have children seek various fish from the ocean or different colored whales instead of pizza toppings. Similar changes can be made to Supermarket Sweep (page 111) and Going to the Zoo (page 113), also in chapter 9. Substitute going to the aquarium and seeking fish. If you are working with a few advanced children, ask questions such as, "What sound is at the end of the word fish?" or "What letters make the 'sh' sound?"

Changing the Space

Activities with Lucy are best suited to a large indoor space with a clean floor surface.

CLASSROOM IDEAS WITH LUCY

Following are some additional activities that feature Lucy as the centerpiece of a unit on whales and oceans. These ideas do not involve movement, but instead incorporate Lucy into other aspects of the curriculum.

- Make reading time extra special by holding it inside Lucy. Read stories that feature whales, fish, or ocean themes. Refer to the

"Resources" section at the end of this chapter for suggested titles about whales written for young children.

- Serve snacks with fish crackers or Jell-O pieces cut out with a fish-shaped cookie cutter. Bring in a fish bowl with real fish for the children to watch swim. If fish are not allowed in your setting, place plastic fish in a fish bowl or small aquarium for the children to watch.
- Fill individual buckets or a sensory table with water and add plastic whales and fish. Let the children play with the plastic toys, simulating fish swimming through the water.
- Purchase or borrow a toy aquarium that comes with plastic marine animals that bob around when the aquarium is switched on. Add a whale and ask the children to identify and share facts about each of the animals.
- Decorate Lucy according to the season. Tape valentines, shamrocks, or pumpkins to her side. Give her a Santa hat on her head and let children feed her candy cane theme cards.
- Record the date Lucy the whale was completed and have a birthday party for her each year. Children—and Lucy—can wear birthday hats. Sing "Happy Birthday" to Lucy and enjoy a snack of fish crackers. Children will love it!

Make Lucy and you can bet young learners will remember this whale of an experience!

RESOURCES

Principal investigator for WhaleNet:

Mr. Michel Williamson
Science Department
Wheelock College, 200 The Riverway, Boston, MA 02215
Phone: 617-879-2256
E-mail: williams@whale.wheelock.edu

Following are stories about whales for young children:

Bunting, E. 2003. *Whales passing.* New York: Blue Sky Press/Scholastic.

Gibbons, G. 1993. *Whales.* Pine Plains, NY: Live Oak Media.

James, S. 1996. *Dear Mr. Blueberry.* New York: Aladdin Press/Simon & Schuster.

Steig, W. 1992. *Amos and Boris.* Valhalla, NY: Sunburst.

chapter 13

Special Events For Program Promotion

Katie smiled as she posed with the chief administrator and some children's parents. The photo was to be run in the local community newspaper. She was smiling because the evening had been particularly successful. The administrator had just congratulated her for conducting an exemplary movement program. The parents seemed genuinely pleased with the movement experiences that their children were receiving. They could see the progress in their children's skills and delighted in the way their children joyfully talked about each movement lesson. Katie had the comforting feeling that she wouldn't have to struggle to justify her equipment purchases next year now that the administration was familiar with her program and its successes. It hadn't been like that two years ago when Katie first came to the program. At that time, administrators, parents, and others knew very little about the children's movement program.

PROGRAM SELF-PROMOTION IS ARGUABLY the single most important thing you can do to assure that the people who are responsible for funding your program recognize its value to the community and continue to fund it at the level needed for success. We encourage you to read the chapter full of easy-to-implement suggestions for program promotion that we share in our first book, *Moving With Purpose* (McCall and Craft 2000). In this chapter we expand on those ideas, focusing on planning and running special events designed to promote your movement program to people who can help you sustain success—key decision makers in your organization, the local community as a whole, and the parents of the children you teach. Program self-promotion can reap great rewards because influential people become familiar with the benefits of all the hard work you and your children do on a daily basis. So make the commitment right now. Do something special to promote your movement program!

The special events discussed in this chapter use timely and seasonal themes as a framework for teaching fitness concepts and movement activities. Children really enjoy the excitement and special attention these events bring to the program. As they come to realize that periodically something special happens in your movement program, they look forward to the next special day. When you make a special effort to organize these events, you are demonstrating to the children that you care about them and what they are doing. This concern further motivates children to stay attentive and involved throughout the year, a great benefit to you as their educator.

When you use these special events to promote your movement program's success, remember to focus your promotion to appeal to your target audience. If you want to gain support for program funding, invite your program director, principal, board members, or chief administrator, and let them see firsthand the value they are already getting for the children in your program. When you need community support or are just interested in educating the community about your program, invite the local media to one of your most interesting and exciting special events. Ask a local personality to lead one of the special events to increase the likelihood that the event might be featured in a one-minute spot on the local evening news. When you want parents to see what their children are achieving, or if you want to increase communication with family adults, be sure to invite them to special events as observers and as volunteers to assist you with the event.

Ten exciting special events are explained in this chapter. Three of them lend themselves to media coverage to inform the community at large about the movement program: Ride for Life, Whale of a Good Time, and All Children Exercising Simultaneously (ACES). Four special events are designed to inform family adults about the movement program and to promote their involvement: Open House, Take a Day to Play, Campaign to Purchase Bike Helmets, and National TV-Turnoff Week. Three others are special activities that generate excitement within the movement program and lend themselves to coverage with a captioned photograph in the community section of the local newspaper: Pumpkin Fun With Families, Ice Skating Party, and Dance Party. We encourage you to try a few of these special events each year until you build a large repertoire of special events. Renée McCall has conducted each of these activities and finds that children love them and learn eagerly through them. As a result, the community awareness and parent support of the Adapted Physical Education Department in the North Syracuse Early Education Program is very high.

Make a commitment to promote your program. At least once a year, invite the local media to report on your most interesting special event. Every few months, send a few photographs with a brief description and an explanation of the event to your local community weekly newspaper for publication. Use these special events to keep everyone aware of the gross motor accomplishments of children in your program. Turn the spotlight of self-promotion on so everyone can see the benefits to children derived from all the hard work you and your children put in each year.

SEPTEMBER: OPEN HOUSE

Schools and child care centers typically hold an open house for family adults, but not their children, during September. Use this open house to give a great first impression.

The following comments are especially pertinent to physical educators. Too often physical educators find that the movement or physical education program is a neglected part of the open house, relegated to the gymnasium in a far corner of the school and unvisited by the throngs of family adults attending that evening. Take action to move your program front and center by staffing a movement program display table near the main entrance to the school.

- Put together a slide show or video presentation of children participating in movement program activities. If it is too early in the school year to gather footage from this year's program, show slides or videotape footage from the previous year. This introduces everyone to activities that children will be doing during the upcoming year. Accompany the video with background music such as the song "Anything I Dream" on the *Minnie 'n Me* CD. (Refer to chapter 3 for order information.)

- Display a photo album that highlights past special events.
- Provide a handout to visiting family adults that outlines the Early Childhood Movement Curricular Goals in chapter 1 on pages 10-11, an overview of the curriculum, and other information about the movement program you wish to share. Include safety requests of parents in the handout such as, "Please have your child wear rubber-soled shoes in which he or she can run safely," and, "Provide a bike helmet for your child to wear during the cycling unit."
- Display adapted equipment that accommodates children's various positioning and mobility needs to reassure parents of children with special needs that their children are indeed included in each movement lesson.
- Finally, add a tablecloth and an arrangement of flowers to provide the finishing touches to the display table.

OCTOBER: PUMPKIN FUN WITH FAMILIES

If you put some effort into the September open house, family adults are likely to have a great first impression of your program. Now you will want to keep them visiting your program throughout the coming months. Invite them to participate in their children's movement program during a week of fun with pumpkins in October.

A typical classroom curriculum for young children includes the celebration of autumn with pumpkins, whether through a field trip to a pumpkin patch or a delivery of pumpkins to the school or center. Coordinate the movement curriculum with these classroom activities. Then invite parents back to visit during their children's movement class. Add a special week to your program in which movement activities revolve around the theme of pumpkins. Refer to Pumpkins Galore in chapter 8 on page 86 for a plethora of activity station ideas using real and plastic pumpkins. Ask to use some of the pumpkins from the pumpkin patch or pumpkin delivery for the activities. Then plan stations that are manageable given your activity space and the number of adults you have available for supervision. Here are some ideas for helping family adults feel welcome and comfortable while visiting your program:

- Send an announcement home a week ahead of time inviting family adults to visit during the week of Pumpkin Fun With Families. Conduct the activities over a week, rather than a single day. This, together with the advance notice, increases the likelihood that many family adults can arrange their work schedules so they can attend on one of the days when their child has movement class.
- Conduct a normal movement lesson with a few changes. Welcome any visiting adults and ask their children to introduce them at the beginning of the lesson. Encourage adults to sit next to their children at the beginning of the lesson and participate in all of the activities with their children. Visiting adults are likely to be unsure about what they are to do during the lesson, so put them at ease. Encourage children to act as hosts to their family adults by inviting them to participate. Use statements such as, "Namgel, please tell your daddy he is welcome to jump with us."
- Children may be extra active and may forget to follow the rules because of their eagerness to show off for their parents. When this happens, reassure the parent that it is very common for a child to misbehave when his or her parent is in the room. Ask the parent's permission to remind the child of the rules. This enables you to maintain your position as the teacher and lets the parent see that you do not allow his or her child to misbehave. You may find that the parent later thanks you in private for addressing the behavior.
- Plan a lesson that requires only general supervision so you can spend a few moments visiting with each parent, sharing information and answering questions. At the end of the lesson, encourage all of the children to say thank you to their visitors and to invite them to come again.
- Consider taking photos of visiting adults as they participate in activities with their children. Then display these on a bulletin board for all to see. Parents soon start to anticipate these monthly activities and look for their photographs on the bulletin board. In this way you establish an invaluable line of communication with families while also promoting your movement program.

NOVEMBER: TAKE A DAY TO PLAY

With a few months of school now behind you, hold an event in November to bring family adults back to your program for more fun. Invite them to come to their child's preschool or primary school program and participate with their son or daughter during at least one movement class during the month for Take a Day to Play. Include a schedule of classes in

the invitation and invite parents to attend any or every class during the month. Let visiting adults see that you are promoting to their children the lifelong habit of warming up, exercising vigorously during the main lesson activity, and then cooling down afterward, the way adults do. Just about any of the activities in this book could be used in these lessons. Give family adults a certificate of participation. Children will love it. If there are children who won't be having a parent or family member coming in sometime that month, ask a member of the staff to be their buddy. Take photos and make a bulletin board of this special time for all to see.

DECEMBER: ICE SKATING PARTY

December is a great time to have an ice skating party. Send an adorable photo of young children enjoying this winter event to the community paper to publish. This special event is briefly explained under Cheap Skate in chapter 4 on page 44. Children put on milk carton or stocking ice skates and twirl around the activity room floor pretending they are professional skaters during this special day. Decorate the area as elaborately as possible to create the atmosphere of a skating rink. Post a sign reading "Skating Rink" at the entrance. Create a warming hut by placing a plastic playhouse in the middle of the skating rink. If no playhouse is available, use a large appliance box that the children have decorated.

Place artificial evergreen trees around which the children can skate. Make your own evergreen trees by taping strips of crepe paper on the sides of large traffic cones. Place large plastic snowmen and reindeer, bought on clearance after the winter holidays, throughout the rink. These obstacles increase the challenge for young skaters and subtly discourage running around the rink. Place a "No Skating" sign next to any restricted areas where children are not to wander. Pretend that this is an outdoor rink and let children wear winter scarves or any other play dress for the occasion. Put on the CD *Waldteufel: The Skater's Waltz* (produced by Nimbus Records and available through www.amazon.com), and let the skating begin.

You can further enhance the wintry feeling by providing a sleigh ride for children. This option is only practical if you have sufficient adult assistance. Use an old laundry cart or wagon decorated to look like a sleigh. Pull the cart or wagon full of children around the perimeter of the skating rink. Children have a great time waving to each other, jingling sleigh bells as they go. We are not aware of any educational purpose in the sleigh ride. It is just a lot of fun. Hot chocolate makes a great seasonal snack at the culmination of the ice skating party.

JANUARY: CAMPAIGN TO PURCHASE BIKE HELMETS

January is a great time to organize a campaign that enables families to order inexpensive bike helmets. Conducting this campaign in the winter ensures that everyone will have a helmet when you start the cycling lessons described in chapter 10 in the spring. Make it part of the year's routine and thus easy to remember to do. For those states still in knee-deep snow, ordering bike helmets in January is a pleasant reminder that spring is coming. For those warmer states where children are able to cycle outdoors during the winter, it is a great month to make and keep the resolution to promote bike helmet safety. Start the New Year off safely with every child's head protected with a helmet while riding a tricycle or bicycle. The campaign is a community service that helps keep the children in your program riding safely while also bringing positive visibility to your movement program.

As discussed in greater detail on pages 145-146 in chapter 10, the campaign consists of providing the opportunity for families to purchase bike helmets for their children at the affordable cost of $5 plus shipping and handling. To conduct the campaign, follow these steps:

- Send home to families promotional flyers for purchasing helmets, complete with order forms and the deadline for returning forms and payment.
- Collate individual orders and place the bulk order with the helmet company.
- Receive the shipment of helmets and organize them for distribution to families.

FEBRUARY: RIDE FOR LIFE

February is National Heart Month, which makes it a great month for emphasizing to your children the importance of cardiovascular fitness. Introduce the *HeartPower!* curriculum and other activities described in chapter 11 into your movement program to get them "pumped up" about health and fitness. Then consider sponsoring a Ride for Life physical fitness and fund-raising event at your school or center.

Ride for Life, described in *Moving With a Purpose* (McCall and Craft 2000, 176), is an excellent way to bring media attention to your program and further promote the benefits of an active lifestyle. Ride for Life consists of children riding their tricycles, bicycles, or other mobility equipment continuously for 25 minutes. The event is held over one or two days,

or longer if necessary, so that every child in your movement program has the opportunity to participate. You can conduct it in a large indoor room or outdoors on a firm surface. Decorate the area like a racetrack with banners and streamers or whatever is at hand to create a festive atmosphere (McCall and Craft 2000). Invite your local police, ambulance personnel, or safety patrol workers to present and distribute pamphlets and other educational resource materials to promoting cycling safety. This event lends itself to a photo of a child cycling and a caption explaining the Ride for Life event. Be sure to ask your community newspaper to provide coverage.

If you choose to sponsor an organization, the fund-raising is accomplished by having children and their families ask people to donate $1 or more to sponsor them as they pedal during the designated time. All children receive certificates of participation for their efforts.

Hold this special event just once a year. Midway through the school year is an excellent time to conduct the Ride for Life because young children are beginning to experience success pedaling and are eager to show off their new skills. National Bike Safety Awareness Month (May) is also a good time to conduct the Ride for Life as the culmination of a unit on cycling safety. The May date provides a chance to be sure that the children have absorbed all the cycling safety information repeated throughout the year and are prepared for a safe summer vacation.

You may also want to arrange a Ride for Life event to promote cardiovascular fitness and safe pedaling, bring positive publicity to your program, and assist in funding heart disease research. The North Syracuse Early Education Program currently conducts the Ride for Life in partnership with the local Onondaga County Health Department Healthy Heart Coalition. Ride for Life has been very well received and supported by parents, children, and the community. For further information or assistance in getting started, contact the North Syracuse Early Education Program, Adapted Physical Education Department, North Syracuse NY 13212, phone 315-452-3024.

MARCH: WHALE OF A GOOD TIME

Lucy the whale is a 55-foot (20 m) inflatable whale that you can build using simple materials from a local hardware store (see chapter 12 for details on how to purchase instructions). Lucy can be the centerpiece for a wonderful special event that is sure to thrill both young children and adults and also bring positive media attention to your program. The activities A Day on the Ocean and A Day at the Beach, both described in chapter 12, work well for spotlighting Lucy. Invite local reporters to your setting to cover the welcoming and first use of Lucy the whale. In North Syracuse, New York, the materials to make Lucy were donated by the parent teacher organization (PTO). She was built by high school students as a science and math project and is now used in teaching preschool children. Local media were invited to cover the story, and two papers carried stories and photos highlighting the collaborative effort. Lucy the whale can serve as a catalyst for great media exposure for your program too!

APRIL: NATIONAL TV-TURNOFF WEEK

Every April an organization called TV-Turnoff Network sponsors National TV-Turnoff Week to encourage families to turn off their televisions and find alternative forms of entertainment. Take the challenge with the young children in your program—and their families—and turn off those televisions. This can be a great time to conduct a weekend afternoon of active pastimes for families in your community. Use the national momentum of this special week to help children find active alternatives to watching television. In doing so you will underscore the importance of the movement program you offer through your efforts to promote healthier, more active lifestyles among the children you teach.

At the beginning of National TV-Turnoff Week, send home a contract for families to complete, stating how much television watching the family is willing to eliminate from their typical viewing schedule during this special week. Give a certificate of participation to those families who successfully complete the challenge and return the signed contract to the school or center. Create a bulletin board at school to display the names of all the families who completed the challenge. Refer families to the great Web site at http://tvturnoff.org for ideas of physical activities to do at home during National TV-Turnoff Week and throughout the year.

Ask the PTO, board of directors, or other governing body in your organization to organize the weekend afternoon of activities for families. Invite families to play games, take part in activities, and attend workshops full of alternatives to watching television. Arrange for several adults in the school, center, or community to work with you in offering this afternoon of active alternatives.

MAY: ALL CHILDREN EXERCISING SIMULTANEOUSLY

May is National Physical Fitness Month. Celebrate it by participating in All Children Exercising Simultaneously (ACES). ACES is an excellent way to bring attention to the importance for regular physical activity. Join many thousands of children across the world in celebrating ACES by performing some form of vigorous exercise from 10:00 to 10:15 a.m. local time on the first Wednesday in May. Over 50 countries and many millions of children participate annually. Organize a school- or center-wide event in which everyone participates in 15 minutes of vigorous exercise.

The following is quoted from *Moving With a Purpose* (McCall and Craft 2000, 174-175).

> ACES is an international program designed to get as many children in the world as possible exercising at the same time. [Over 50 countries and many millions of children participate annually.] It was started in 1989 by Len Saunders, a physical educator at Valley View School, Montville, New Jersey. The program takes place from 10:00 to 10:15 a.m. on the first Wednesday in May. Each school organizes its own event with children doing any form or combination of exercise, including walking, running, dancing, calisthenics, and aerobics. Exercises and aerobic movements to music work well with preschool children and include children who require adapted mobility equipment. Here is a list of suggestions to make preschool children's participation in ACES a success:
>
> ***In advance***
>
> - Send home fliers promoting the event, inviting friends and family to participate.
> - Decorate bulletin boards around the building promoting the event.
> - Invite local media to cover the event.
> - Invite local personalities to participate.
> - Arrange for an adult personality at the school or center to dress as a cartoon character or as the school mascot.
> - Select theme music for each year. Plan musical movement songs and decorations that reflect each year's theme.
>
> ***During the event***
>
> - Have energizing music playing as the children enter the large room for the event.
> - Play the national anthem just prior to 10:00 a.m.
> - Hold up large numbered cards to lead children in the countdown to begin exercising.
> - Play high-energy music throughout the 15 minutes. Five songs will typically fill the 15 minutes. Invite a variety of staff or students to lead the audience in musical movement activities.
> - Use visual cue cards, especially with a large audience, to tell the audience and performers what to do. Hold up the

cue card stating "Touch your toes" for example, as the exercise calls for toe touches.

- Designate a master of ceremony to keep the event running smoothly and the audience aware of what is happening next.
- Distribute certificates to participants at the end of the event.

This can be a great event. [Go to the web site members.aol.com/acesday to learn more about the event.] Get involved and participate!*

JUNE: DANCE PARTY

*Reprinted, by permission, from R. McCall and D. Craft, 2000, *Moving with a purpose: Developing programs for preschoolers of all abilities* (Champaign, IL: Human Kinetics), 174-175.

The end of the school year is a great time to invite family adults to visit your program as their children celebrate the beginning of summer with a dance party! Organize the activities and decorate the area to create a festive environment.

- Make or buy paper crowns for each child to wear.
- If you wish, set up a garden area for adults to take pictures of their children at the dance.
- Have a designated area where people can line up to request music.
- Have musical movement wands available (curling ribbon tied around a pipe cleaner, twisted into a circle for grasping), for each child to use during the party and then to take home.
- Play familiar music with dictated action movements that children can imitate.
- Use this time to stress to visiting adults the importance of dancing and other forms of physical activity.

Set a designated time for the party to begin and end, perhaps after 30 or 45 minutes. A good thing can go bad if it continues too long. This is particularly true with young children.

We hope you find joy and purpose as you play these low-cost activities with the young children in your movement program.

References

American Automobile Association (AAA) Traffic Safety Services. 1998. *Kids speak out on bike helmets.* Washington, DC: American Automobile Association.

Baby Einstein. 2002. Buena Vista (compact disc).

Comprehensive Health Education Foundation. 1995. *Primarily health series: Feeling fit, That's it! teacher's guide.* Bothell, WA: Wright Group.

McCall, R., and D. Craft. 2000. *Moving with a purpose: Developing programs for preschoolers of all abilities.* Champaign, IL: Human Kinetics.

Miles, E. 1997. *Tune your brain.* New York: Berkeley Books.

Moomaw, S. 1997. *More than singing: Discovering music in preschool and kindergarten.* St. Paul, MN: Redleaf Press.

Motion series: Volume one. 2001. Mayatek, Inc. (compact disc).

National Association for Sport & Physical Education. 2000. *Appropriate practices in movement programs for young children ages 3–5.* Reston, VA: NASPE Publications.

National Association for Sport & Physical Education. 2004. *Moving into the future: National standards for physical education: A guide to content.* New York: McGraw-Hill.

Pica, R. 1999. Music and the movement program. *Teaching Elementary Physical Education, 10* (4): 32-33.

U.S. Surgeon General. 2001. *2001 Surgeon General's call to action to prevent and decrease overweight and obesity.* Retrieved November 14, 2003, from http://www.surgeongeneral.gov/topics/obesity/calltoaction/fact_adolescents.htm.

Weikert, P. 1997. *Movement plus rhymes, songs, and singing games.* 2d ed. Ypsilanti, MI: High/Scope Educational Research Foundation.

About the Authors

Renee M. McCall, MS, is a certified adapted physical educator who teaches in the Early Education Program at North Syracuse (New York) Central School District. McCall has been teaching preschool adapted physical education since 1985. Among her awards are those for the 2003 Adapted Physical Activity Council National Adapted Physical Education Program of the Year and the 2002 New York State Health Department's Award of Excellence. The latter recognizes the most outstanding preschool for promotion of health and fitness in young children.

McCall is an adjunct instructor at the State University of New York (SUNY) at Cortland. Her articles on teaching have been published in both the *Journal of Health, Physical Education, Recreation and Dance* and *Teaching Elementary Physical Education*.

Diane H. Craft, PhD, is a professor in the department of physical education at State University of New York (SUNY) at Cortland. She teaches adapted physical education and supervises practica providing physical education instruction to individuals with disabilities.

Craft is a past president of the National Consortium of Physical Education and Recreation for Individuals with Disabilities (NCPERID). Previously, she devoted 10 years to directing U.S. Department of Education federal training grants in physical education. An experienced elementary and high school physical education teacher, Craft is a committed advocate of the inclusion of children with disabilities in general physical education classes.

McCall and Craft also cowrote *Moving with a Purpose: Developing Programs for Preschoolers of All Abilities*, to which *Purposeful Play* is a companion book. The authors are highly acclaimed speakers who have conducted many presentations and workshops at state, national, and international events. They also have contributed to training videos for early childhood educators across New York State.